Let Me Give It To You Straight

An Outspoken Guide to Working With
Headhunters, Advancing Your Career
and Reaching Enlightenment . . .
Without the Sugarcoating

Mark Jaffe

CGW
PUBLISHING

2014

Let Me Give It To You Straight

An Outspoken Guide to Working With Headhunters, Advancing Your Career and Reaching Enlightenment . . . Without the Sugarcoating

First Edition: November 2014

ISBN 978-1-9082933-1-2

CGW Publishing 2014

CGW Publishing

B1502

PO Box 15113

Birmingham

B2 2NJ

United Kingdom

www.cgwpublishing.com

mail@cgwpublishing.com

Let Me Give It To You Straight

1

JOIN ME FOR LUNCH?

The world of commerce is simultaneously modern and medieval, technological and primitive. Its ancient rituals can seem infused with Divine Light as they guide our steps. Social media also helps. Wealth, power, glamour, fame . . . having the best tax attorney in New York. It makes me want to put on a tie for lunch! And yet there's nothing I know of that strips the varnish *off* business and its heroes like executive search. If you enjoy seeing people at their most vulnerable, please fill out our application.

The search profession was a spin-off, shortly after World War II, of the management consulting profession. Search was a sub-specialty, and its practitioners labored tirelessly to ensure that the public regarded them as consultant-advisors, not salesmen. Moreover it was an image business, and in their efforts to appear whitest-of-bread and bluest-of-blood, executive recruiters single-handedly elevated Brooks Brothers to the status of megabrand.

A client's hiring agenda can vary broadly, anywhere from status quo ("Fred dropped dead at his desk this morning. Can you bring us somebody just like him by end of day?") to bold and game-changing ("We want to break all the dishes. Seriously. But without upsetting anyone."). Since corporations are tribal in nature, the first rule is to find candidates they recognize as their own kind. Even more challenging is when management clings to an unrealistic self-image and insists on dating only supermodels.

Our assignments *are* reminiscent of a beauty pageant. In an effort to provide clients with the illusion of choice, we internalize their business goals and express that understanding through the recruitment of multiple candidates, each one differing slightly from the next. In the old days when the word 'Rolodex' was commonly heard, the trick was to have a broad network of contacts with expertise in specific industries and functions. The game has changed, though; now everyone is visible. So it comes down to our good taste and judgment: how we handicap the players, how we package the opportunity and how we manage the recruitment process.

The people we approach are almost never looking for a change. They are, but they don't know it yet. We do research to identify who we want by experience and reputation. The prospects, in turn, field our phone calls and pretend to be ambivalent. Believe me, no one is fooled. You can sit around and wait to be promoted . . . or you can take the bait and go to the interview.

Search people are functionally comparable to psychotherapists. We get to ask impertinent questions, probe and poke around to our heart's content, then make our diagnosis. Unlike mental health professionals, we don't aspire to improve the subject's condition. Just the opposite! We are bound by the charter of our mission to sit in judgment, to be vigilant gatekeepers and to prevent the unworthy from entering Paradise. Then we go someplace nice for lunch.

In our culture – possibly even in the Bolivian rainforest – there exists a kind of social contract that defines how we look at each other, thereby limiting what we see. You don't stare at someone when he is digging in his ear or picking his nose or fumbling, painfully, for the next word to answer a question. Awkward, uncomfortable moments, flashes of uncertainty – when we encounter these in others we reflexively glance away, giving the person a moment to reorganize his presentation. It's only polite. Your empathy kicks in, together with your willingness to uphold convention. Plainly stated: you don't want to see the person naked because you don't like to be exposed, either.

There are several situations, however, where the usual rules are suspended and we allow others to observe us from a more holistic perspective. At the doctor's office, before being examined, you must literally and symbolically remove your garments so as to be more thoroughly inspected. We agree to this, don't we? All bets are off, then, about camouflaging a mole or covering up that sexy new tattoo. The game is a bit more sophisticated, sprinkled with an element of hide-and-go-seek, perhaps, at the analyst's office. But the principle remains: you're there to be viewed. Ditto if you go for a massage. You actually *want* the masseuse to find your hidden tension, right?

Another common situation in which we present ourselves for viewing is the formal interview. While it may be part performance (you'll probably go with every intention of maintaining a bulletproof façade), it's fully understood by both parties that there will be a fair dose of scrutiny – or deep looking – as part of the ceremony. The fact is that you're putting yourself on display and granting someone permission to 'view' you.

Know what 'Oz' stands for? Outer Zone. The false self we project. Every person is a little like Frank Morgan, nervously exhorting, "Pay no attention to that man behind the curtain! I am the great and powerful Wizard of Oz!" My job – for whatever it's worth – is to gain *access* to the person behind the curtain, to *grasp* who that individual truly is (within the context of my objectives) and to *translate* that perception into valuable advice for my clients. All knowledge must lead to action. And then we go someplace nice for lunch.

Join me. I'll expense it.

2

AH, YESTERDAY!

Remember when you were little, say, second or third grade, and you stayed home from school on a biting cold winter day with a sore throat and a fever? Your mom would come in and put her lips to your forehead. Then, just to be sure, she'd take your temperature. Maybe she'd fluff your pillows, too, or bring you that satin and goose down comforter she saved for special occasions. Chances are she'd roll the television into your room on its portable stand with those noisy wheels and adjust the rabbit ears so you could watch *I Love Lucy* followed by *My Little Margie*.

Every mom had her own special elixir for dealing with a cold or the flu. Mine used to make warm eggnog with vanilla and a dash of nutmeg. There were board games in the afternoon when soap operas ruled the airwaves. If she had time, she might read a story from Kipling or from Edith Hamilton's *Mythology*.

Well, this is nothing like that. Not even close. It's more like that prison in *Midnight Express*, but without the friendly guards. Or the worst paper-cut ever. Or spontaneous human combustion, where a person's clothing soaks up liquefied fat from the body and acts as a giant wick. Yeow.

What I'm trying to say here is that things are very bad. One minute you leave for work, shouting, "I'll see you at six!" Next thing you know, your hedge fund manager is on the phone explaining that it's not personal. Incredibly, he has the nerve to quote Kafka: "Oh, plenty of hope, an infinite amount of hope – but not for *us*."

Roger that.

Then it really starts to deteriorate. Even the dog seems resentful. Just when you were beginning to accept the idea that you'd never completely conquer the world, the bottom drops out. You find yourself wondering how many days in a row you can wear the same socks. Who would care?

It's not the like the high times, the fat years. Nothing compared to, say, 2002. Back then you could sail along in your upgraded aisle seat and perhaps wind up chatting with a famous entrepreneur or a television weather guy. You, the capitalist with the soul of a poet. You were going somewhere then! You were doing *business!* Oh, the bitter irony of that word now. The horror.

Slow down the roller coaster for a minute, you keep thinking. It's all unraveling so quickly. Let's not focus on whether we deserved the privilege and the status and the smooth ride, shall we? Can't we have it back and *then* discuss it? This is clearly not your grandfather's famine – if only! Tales of the Great Potato Thingy are being conjured up in tones of warm nostalgia. Life was good, wasn't it?

Compared to this, seventh-grade gym class felt like a cool breeze on a sunny afternoon. Run the laps. Climb the rope. Get hit with the wet towel. Smell the coffee. Smell the roses. Smell the coffee-scented roses. Get hit with another wet towel. Ah, yesterday!

And now, with every conceivable weakness exposed, a single truth remains: No one knows anything. We may soon be facing the largest Decompression in the history of mankind and what has been done to stop it? Nada. Enjoy whatever time you have left.

But consider the possibility that we're looking at our current situation through the wrong end of the telescope. What if this was some kind of mystical growth opportunity for everyone, a chance to evolve emotionally and spiritually during a material low ebb? How could we harness that potential?

Maybe all we need is a giant dose of optimism, a shot of 'can do' so potent it would make Frank Capra blush. If we were to assume that a basic value is to avoid standing around waiting for something good to happen, perhaps we should each take a personal minute to ask: "Am I closer to this worthy ideal than when I woke up this morning?"

Or, alternatively . . . things could just be *very, very bad.*

You're not going to hear me say that hardship, uncertainty, deprivation and unemployment will make you a better person. No way am I going to mindlessly echo the platitude that whatever doesn't kill you makes you stronger. That's not how I roll.

I don't know about you, but I want my Mommy.

3

WHAT DOES A HEADHUNTER REALLY LOOK FOR IN A CANDIDATE?

"The great question that has never been answered, and which I have not yet been able to answer, despite my thirty years of research into the feminine soul, is 'What does a woman want?'"

Sigmund Freud

Freud had a pretty smooth gig. Here was a man who enticed wealthy, neurotic women to his office and – relaxing their inhibitions with hypnosis – encouraged them to describe their fantasies while lying on his chaise lounge. As if that wasn't enough, he profitably published these sessions . . . and then billed them. Still, he didn't completely get it.

We have the same problem lately with leadership. It's the hottest topic for business books of every shape and flavor, yet despite all the 'five qualities this' and 'seven characteristics that,' we still don't get it, either. Honestly, isn't it a bit like pornography? We can't really define it, but we know it when we see it.

Perhaps leaders are simply labeled as such *after the fact* by what they've done. We see their trail of smoke and know in our hearts that they delivered, like the Lone Ranger. There are a few telltale hints along the way: balance sheets, stock prices, looking at who and how they hire – but mostly it's not over until the fat lady sings.

Another big question about executives in general is whether past accomplishments are even marginally a predictor of future performance in a new environment. The smart money says, "Don't hold your breath." Equally mysterious – although recruiters never stop bragging about their abilities in this area – is the art or science of reliably indicating 'fit' between candidate and corporate 'culture.'

So let's review what *can't* be substantiated: leadership whatever-it-is, portability of success, compatibility with a pre-existing group. These are the great unknowns, depending as they do on time, situation and sheer luck. So what can we know? What do we at least look for?

Here's what it boils down to, in my humble opinion:

First, we like to see a strong reputation within a given industry. People work together, people talk. Independent of anything else, a killer rep can open doors and move mountains. We instinctively give the benefit of the doubt to someone who has been rumored to produce the occasional miracle. And if nobody much has ever heard of you, we're inclined to suspect there may be good reason.

Next, we're holding a cool hand of cards if our candidate demonstrates impeccable character and integrity, both in our eyes and in those of her colleagues. Does the outside match what we see inside? Is she speaking from a place of authenticity, or is she 'spoon feeding' us warmed-over advertisements for herself? Further, can we identify a track record of this person making tough and not always popular decisions? Does she walk the talk? Obviously we rely heavily on references for perspective, and I don't mean references the candidate has provided.

Finally, the all-important and most elusive piece: seemingly relevant achievements or victories in what may (or may not) be comparable settings. Each business endeavor comes with its own set of values and challenges. There has never been an empirical scale by which we could gauge the potential worth of individuals to corporations. Please mistrust anyone who says there is.

Likewise, there is no consistent baseline or yardstick that factors in *everything:* track record, age, gender, education, sector, market conditions, rank, compensation, internal resources, company politics, reliance on outside relationships . . . the list goes on and on. Literally dozens of elements may impact an executive's success.

So we try to build a case – to find convincing parallels – even though our evidence is purely circumstantial. The best we can do is tally up as many clues as possible to persuade ourselves that lightning could reasonably strike again, if fate so decrees.

Maybe it's like the story about the man who's on his hands and knees, searching the ground under a streetlight. His friend walks by and says, "What are you doing there?"

"Looking for my car keys," he answers.

"Where did you see them last?" the friend asks.

"Around the corner."

"Then why are you looking here?"

"Duh," he says. "Because it's *light* here."

I can't speak for anyone else, but I've personally had it with getting ahead in business on good looks alone. Just once, I'd like it to be about the quality of the work.

Unique aspect of service. Elegant delivery. Lasting value. Put these elements together and you have a recipe that's close to magic. With magic, it's not about convincing people to watch you do your tricks. It's about doing tricks so well that people ask you — over and over again — to keep doing them.

4

STOP READING CAREER ADVICE COLUMNS

Having just finished an article by a popular syndicated columnist entitled, *7 Things You Should Never Wear to an Office Party,* a couple of things occur to me. First, do I have enough medication in the house to kill myself? And second, why isn't everyone tired of career advice yet?

It's as if every high school guidance counselor and employment agency manager who ever lived was awakened – perhaps by some kind of ultrasonic alarm from a passing spacecraft – and huddled together from lonely graves the world over, platoon-like, to attack us. In short, a zombie picture.

You can imagine it, too, I'm sure. Directed by M. Night Shyamalan or the Coen brothers, the plot would hinge on who can discover the zombies' hidden weakness and shrewdly exploit it to save what's left of our ravaged civilization. Probably a resourceful twelve year-old girl. Through a suspenseful process of trial and error – alluded to in ancient, pre-internet manuscripts as Real Life Experience – our unlikely heroine will discover that her own observations are *at least* as valuable as the blurbs she picks up at Yahoo! Finance on how to market her youthfulness to its maximum advantage. (Her mother, of course, will be played by Jodie Foster.)

Seriously, what do you suppose makes an otherwise sane individual take counsel from a media edutainment specialist on the subject of what to say at the next product launch meeting? Is it all just anyone's guess? During one of those years of the Great Internet Boom I heard an urban legend – pretty sure it was a news story on NPR – about an enterprising group of scientists who threw darts at listings of stock symbols in a controlled experiment and yielded, overall, slightly better returns than the leading market analysts. Is the lesson here that no one knows anything . . . ever? Is that why professionalism is currently up for grabs? Could be. The reason tall tales like this endure, clearly, is because of their total believability.

Are you reasonably good at what you do? Has anyone besides you and your mother, spouse or career coach noticed? In my forthcoming book, *Less Is More: Please Tell the Emperor His Suit Is Ready*, I bravely examine the widespread phenomenon of corporate insecurity . . . and reach the inevitable conclusion that it's everywhere. (Groundbreaking stuff; watch for it on Amazon.) What it means in practical terms is that only one in ten people will operate with confidence, while the other 90% will continue to worry about whether someone else might be doing it better.

Contrary to popular belief, *there are no success secrets;* the important stuff is all painfully obvious. I hope my readers, if any, will eventually come to realize that it's about experience, performance, maturity and attitude rather than techniques, protocol, gimmicks and magic talismans. Although four out of five users report that reading my essays is more satisfying than actually being with me, there is *no scientific evidence* that anything I write has demonstrable value. As my father, of blessed memory, used to say, "If it was easy, then everyone would do it."

In high school I knew someone who had a solid reputation for cutting class and spending occasional short stints in the local reformatory. He used to do a marvelous trick. He would blow one monster smoke ring and before it dissipated, he'd shoot ten little ones right through its center. I still consider myself fortunate to have seen it with my own eyes. As impressive as it was, nothing aside from the memory ever remained of this unique accomplishment. Where is he now? Probably federal penitentiary. Or writing a career advice column for CNBC.

5

THERE ARE NO SAFE JOBS – PERHAPS THERE NEVER WERE

In case you didn't notice, things have changed. Not just the big stuff, like unemployment, net-worth shrinkage and that scary, mysterious deep-sea monster called 'globalization.' I'm referring to the subtle but fundamental changes that affect your job, your professional status and what we used to call your 'career trajectory.' Welcome to the New Order.

To begin with, forget whatever you may have believed about 'levels' of progress. Levels don't exist anymore . . . and maybe never did, except in your mind. It doesn't matter if you were a superstar five years or even five months ago. This is Instant Karma. You might have achieved dizzying heights in an earlier lifetime, but lately it's all in the Right Now.

What does that mean? It means you can drink coffee, but you can't really go 'on break.' It means there is little or no leveraging of previous accomplishments. Yes, I said that. Past performance has been hammered as flat as your retirement account. Crazy, huh? You say you slew the dragon and saved an entire village from destruction? When was that, last week? Fuhgeddaboudit. We're over it, and you need to get over it, too. Try proving your value *today*.

If every single morning at work feels like an audition for a play that is yet to be written, you've got the idea.

Loyalty, as I'm sure you've come to realize, hasn't been worth anything for a long time. And it's worth significantly less now. If we don't care what you did last week, why would your 17 years of tireless service be a matter of interest? The assumption is that you're coasting . . . so get to work!

Ah, work. Again, I advise you to watch your back. Get ready to be judged not on productivity, but on popularity. This isn't an original observation. Pragmatists have been no doubt warning idealists for countless centuries that existence in general and enterprise in particular are not meritocracies. When actress Meryl Streep addressed the 1983 graduating class at Vassar, she cautioned that real life is not like college:

"Real Life is actually a lot more like high school. The common denominator prevails. Excellence is not always recognized or rewarded. What we watch on our screens, whom we elect, are determined to a large extent by public polls. Looks count. A lot. And unlike the best of the college experience, when ideas and solutions somehow seem attainable if you just get up early, stay up late, try hard enough, and find the right source or method, things on the outside sometimes seem vast and impossible, and settling, resigning oneself, or hiding and hunkering down becomes the best way of getting along."

More talented writers than yours truly have been quick to note a recent leap in visibility of this rather shabby metaphysical truth. Not only should you avoid telling co-workers (and others) what you think is lacking, people also need to feel that you basically like them. As Colonel Cathcart and Colonel Korn told Yossarian in *Catch 22*, "Just *like* us! We're not bad guys! All you have to do is *like* us!"

Since no one appears to know what's going to succeed and what isn't business-wise, your communication *style* is now far more important than *what* you have to say. People don't value your input nearly so much as your cooperation. Simply stated, it's all about three things:

1. The other person.

2. What you can do for them.

3. How you make them feel about themselves.

Any advice on how to handle these sweeping changes without going insane? There are probably a number of techniques and I invite readers to share them with us. I can tell you what works for me: I don't expect to be taken seriously. Yup, that's it. And maybe you shouldn't, either. Groucho often said, "If you find it hard to laugh at yourself, I'd be happy to do it for you."

6

HOW TO IDENTIFY AUTHENTIC LEADERS

It's been said that there are two types of people: the ones who say that there are two types of people . . . and the ones who don't. My version of this classic theme is that people tend to either play to their own strengths or burn up an equal amount of energy protecting their weaknesses.

It should come as no surprise that candidates at the upper echelons of management interview beautifully. Nearly everyone who makes enormous bucks will have crisp, compelling answers to all the toughest interview questions. And a powerful person with well-rehearsed, polished material is generally able to spin a story just about any way the situation requires.

How do executive recruiters get to see the man or woman beyond the gilded resume and the facile business-speak? That's a topic for another time, possibly a whole mini-series. What are we even looking for when we *do* penetrate the wrapping paper? Let's start with our two types, the strength and weakness people.

Forget the impressive track record of personal accomplishments and increasingly impressive levels of responsibility for a minute. Never mind how impeccably dressed, articulate and engaging the person may be. Here's an obvious window from which you can begin to look at whether an executive is operating from a set of authentic competencies or attempting to mask their own vulnerabilities: *who and how that person hires.*

Ah, the summer of '84 – it seems like only yesterday. Rocks were still soft, moss had just begun to grow on trees and I was starting out in the search business. I don't recall whether it was during my first day, week or month, but at some point I was taught the Cardinal Rule of Search: 'A' players hire 'A' players – and 'B' players hire 'C' players. It made sense in theory. Until you watch it in action, though, the implications are murky at best.

Then I saw it happen once, twice, a dozen times. Hiring managers would pass on the candidate who showed superstar potential and go with the predictable, boring choice. Low voltage, low risk, low return. Only a special breed of manager had the vision and the confidence to hire people potentially smarter and more talented than himself, and while those hires sometimes failed (as humans sometimes do), the dividends on the ones who succeeded were often spectacular.

Remember "Ozymandias" from high school, the poem by Shelley? If you've been in the corporate world more than 15 minutes, you know exactly how those "vast and trunkless legs of stone" block the road to progress. Enlightened, high-octane leaders capitalize on the innate talents and passions of individuals, including their own, rather than guarding "the lone and level sands."

I don't know about you, but sometimes I think it might be cool to work with a company where people *do* get fired for buying IBM.

7

GET RECRUITERS TO NOTICE YOU – WIN VALUABLE PRIZES!

Assuming that the goal of life for most people is to appear on *American Idol*, a close second may be getting noticed by an executive recruiter. Noticed in a good way, that is.

Sadly, there is no formal protocol. Yet the question is still asked, and legitimately so. Now more than ever before, amidst a torrent of unsolicited resumes raining down on headhunters in the severest of hiring climates, they're being confronted by ambitious people who want to know what the deal is. Spoiler alert: the explanation will prove thoroughly unsatisfying.

There are two approaches to consider. Choose your preferred brand.

Approach One goes like this: Look or sound as if you are someone capable of and likely to dole out tons of search business to the recruiter once he or she installs you in that sleek new corporate role. In other words, exude the whiff of a meal ticket and you'll have the most streetwise consultants dancing around you for their supper.

Approach Two is even more limiting and distinctly unglamorous: Do memorable work in your industry or profession and, despite your employer's best efforts to conceal your brilliance from the rest of the world, we will find you.

Can't I offer something – anything – in the way of constructive detail, you ask? Let's see. It's beyond simple, really. Take on a miserable-but-important project that nobody wants or where others have failed . . . and succeed. It also helps if there's an opportunity for you to make someone else look heroic in the process. Specifically your boss. No self-promoting on company time, either. Act like it's not about you, ever, especially when you hit a home run. You're just – aw, shucks – doing your bit for the old team. And don't hit on the receptionist. She's out of your league.

Sorry to be the bearer of bad news, but that's really it.

8

WHAT TO DO WHEN THE HEADHUNTER CALLS

Everyone seems to have a favorite cold remedy, chili recipe, or sure-fire method for getting lipstick stains off shirt collars. Similarly, there has been a spate of highly assertive articles in recent years on the subject of fielding calls from executive recruiters, with special emphasis on that critical first interface. Kindly accept this as my modest contribution to the genre.

Here is what I believe you should consider:

Decide whether or not you can talk. If it isn't a good time – or you don't have complete privacy – make other arrangements. Too simple, right? And yet you'd be surprised how many people try to communicate in 'code' or innuendo. Don't attempt a cloak-and-dagger conversation if the walls might have ears or your administrative assistant has her phone on mute.

Be sure the recruiter has the right person on the line. Did she call you on purpose, or is she just trolling for warm bodies? Does she roughly know what you do for a living and how to pronounce your name? Ask where she heard about you . . . but don't have a fit if she can't or won't say. See if you can figure out whether it's a fishing expedition or a case of her very specifically targeting your background and skills. If all she wants is information, tell her to call 411.

Ask whether the recruiter is retained, contingency or in-house. Trust me, it makes a huge difference. Are you still fuzzy about these categories? Retained consultants have already been hired and paid by their corporate clients to research, prospect, engage and assess talent for a particular role. They have an exclusive relationship with the company relative to each search assignment.

Contingency recruiters get paid like real estate agents – only when they close a deal. As a result, they tend to be sell sell sell all the way.

Tell me if this sounds familiar: "Roberta? This is Duane Jurkinov at Acme Management Recruiting. Have I got an opportunity for you!" Need I say more?

In-house recruiters work for their companies as captive employees. They have a job to do and an internal constituency to satisfy. Some are terrific, but only a few are truly influential.

You'll want the recruiter to understand that you're not looking (unless you're out of work, of course). You can accomplish this by saying, "Are you under the impression that I'm currently looking or on the market? Because I'm not." Don't overdo it, though. Just mention it and move on.

Get the company name and position title for the job opening. This exchange is not intended to be all give and no take. Provide information, certainly, but expect to receive a proportional amount of information in return. In some instances, you may be told that it's a confidential search. No problem, you say, because you won't discuss it with anyone . . . just like he may not mention you to anyone without your permission. Bottom line: Tell him he can check you out on LinkedIn until the next millennium, but if he wants you to share a resume and provide details on your compensation package, he'd better cough up a name and other pertinent facts.

Find out how long the job's been open and why. Where did the last person go? (Promoted? Left the company? Doesn't know yet that he's being replaced?) To whom does the position report? Who is *that* person's boss? If it's a newly created role, have the recruiter explain the mission. If it's an existing job, ask him to tell you what needs to be improved.

Be clear and precise about your compensation when asked. Only when asked. No lumping; break it down for her: how much base, how much bonus, how much stock and other extras. Don't be coy . . . and *don't lie*. Incidentally, the headhunter doesn't want to hear your opinion of what you *should* be making. Do mention, however, if you have a review coming up or anticipate an increase within the next few months for some other reason.

Have a credible answer ready for the following question: "What would an opportunity have to include – or exclude, for that matter – to make it irresistible to you?" Be transparent and sincere about what's important to you in evaluating any career change.

Offer to send your resume after you see the job spec. Obtain an unequivocal promise that the recruiter will never show it to anyone *ever* unless you give him explicit permission to do so.

Don't play games or waste anyone's time. Like your Mom used to say: "You never get a second chance to make a first impression." Act professional and not like a 14 year-old at a school dance. Chillaxify yourself. It's just a conversation, not a lifelong commitment.

Finally, please remember that headhunters, like lecherous old men, need love, too. (Occasionally it's an overlapping demographic.) The quickest way to ingratiate yourself to a headhunter when he calls is to say the magic words: *"Hold on a second. I need to close my door."*

9

THINGS YOU CAN LEARN FROM A DOG THAT WILL HELP YOUR CAREER

"Outside of a dog, a book is probably man's best friend. Inside of a dog, it's too dark to read."

Groucho Marx

It seems we'll go to any lengths these days to find inspiration and guidance, particularly when it comes to the subject of how to behave at work. Whether it's the cool-headed planning of Machiavelli or the management finesse of Genghis Khan, there's a consistent hunger to know what the Big Dogs know. "Teach us the rules so we can play on your turf!" the new generation demands of the old. As my human resource friends have kindly pointed out, people need help.

But do we really have to reach so far back into history for torches to illuminate the path? I think not. In fact, we may have to look no farther than our own back yards . . . or family sofas. In random order, here are some laudable canine traits, which, if correctly applied, should arouse your nascent (or ailing) career to its fullest potential:

A dog doesn't complain when you wake him. I realize you like to sleep. So does a dog! Still, he embraces each moment − a recurring theme, as we'll soon see − and is ready for action no matter what the clock says.

Regardless of how long it took him to get comfortable, he's not inconvenienced by having to move. Didn't someone once write an inane book about moving the cheese? The point is that certainty and security are illusions. You can do three rotations or 300 before settling in – it makes no difference – but as long as you're working for a company or for yourself, rich or poor, living in society or a hermit . . . there is no safe haven, period. Forget your bobblehead collection or whatever it is and move on to the next thing.

A dog only cares what you say *to* him, not *about* him. Science might one day prove me wrong . . . and I can live with that. In the meantime, I'm confident stating that a dog is not interested in what you think of him – only how you *act*. Since he is never fake or disingenuous, I guess he just takes it for granted that you are equally real. Your opinions don't matter – neither does gossip, slander or innuendo – so there's little chance of him taking offense when your view of him doesn't flatter or match his own. He loves your praise, shrinks from your rebuke and appears to never carry a grudge because he doesn't dwell on the past. What counts for him is *right now*. Don't you wish you knew people like this?

No pants? No problem! Most of us can only imagine what it's like to forget about how we look to others. Even as infants we learn to engineer our public images for maximum effectiveness. A dog will also modify his behavior based on environmental reinforcements, but for him it's all about the result, not the image – which is nothing more than memory with gum on its shoe. He doesn't think he's a big deal or a martyr, either one. No lying, no exaggerating. He just is what he is.

He's there for you, not for you to help him self-actualize. Yeah, it's the loyalty thing. Also known as fidelity, hence the name 'Fido.' If we started looking through this end of the telescope, we'd all be a lot more productive. News flash: Your employer is only interested in what you can do for the business. That doesn't make you a slave or require you to be co-dependent. Find your satisfaction when and where you can get it, but be the dedicated servant while you're at work and watch the dividends accrue. As usual, it's not about you.

Everything and everybody has to pass the smell test. You've seen this a thousand times. A dog gathers robust, highly textured data through his olfactory sense, similar to how a blind person reads Braille or the way Sherlock Holmes seems clairvoyant. You can learn to do it, too. It might be literal or metaphorical; just remember that your brain figures heavily into the equation. Whether sniffing out a compelling proposal or a shapely derrière, ask yourself: Does this smell right? Is something off? Does it all add up? When do we eat?

Take a short power nap. Everything in moderation, right?

10

DANGER! BAD CANDIDATE! RUN AWAY!

In the race for talent, companies should know when to flee in the opposite direction. Given the total cost of what could often be avoidable hiring errors, I advise learning to recognize a few not-so-well-known telltale indicators – and to avoid displaying any of these symptoms if you're a candidate.

Look for the following cautionary signs (and contact local law enforcement if you suspect foul play) while performing due diligence. Prospective hires may be seriously flawed or merely damaged goods if the candidate:

Has difficulty talking off script about non-business topics, and never seems completely natural or unrehearsed. Is there a real person hiding inside? Who, exactly, are you talking to?

Struggles to answer the question, "What wrong turns or tragic decisions have you made in your career?" This demonstrates an inability to do honest, self-critical analysis. Do you want someone who lacks introspection?

During the interview reveals a conspicuous lack of 'crash and burn' experience. Makes it impossible to know how he or she deals with situational failures, setbacks, and disappointments. Will the candidate fold like a cheap suit at the first sign of serious pressure?

Can't identify a work relationship – subordinate, peer, or boss – that became dysfunctional, where the wheels came off. More specifically, is unable to acknowledge or attribute any factors in that breakdown (even marginally) to his or her own behaviors and choices.

Candidate's resume includes unsuccessful attempts at 'consulting.' (Please note the key word, *'unsuccessful.'* As in profitless and maybe even client-less.) Is this nothing more than a camouflage for unemployed? While there's no shame in being between gigs, an effort to mask the truth says something in itself.

Was led at some point by so-called venture capital 'buddies' into one or more start-ups with hollow business plans (i.e., not based on a compelling premise, product, service or technology). What was he or she thinking . . . get rich quick? Maybe not the impulsive profile you want for your organization.

Never mentions 'the team' while relating stories of conquest. It's all and always about me, me and more me.

Alludes to overly cozy relationships with top management, or, in the case of a CEO, with current or past board members. This suggests that the candidate is a shameless name-dropper, and may have been under the 'protective care' of friends in high places (as opposed to actually earning their stripes). Or both.

Men with lacquered fingernails; women with raccoon-like mascara and eyeliner. (Sorry if you disagree, but sometimes my preferences should just become formal legislation.)

Hiring managers shouldn't expect to necessarily catch every red flag, but should seek input and validation from peers and/or assessment consultants whenever possible to ensure that the prospect they are planning to hire is an individual of exceptional substance – and not just a polished self-promoter.

If you're about to sign off on an expensive package for someone, make sure you have the right someone. And if you're a candidate, check the mirror for these potentially fatal imperfections.

11

WHEN BAD RESUMES HAPPEN TO GOOD PEOPLE

If your 401K has dwindled to a 201K and your real estate has gone soft, it's possible that the most important thing you own right now is your resume. But if the flow of emails into my office is any indication, the number of people with bad resumes has reached epidemic proportions. Worse, they don't understand why I'm not doing back flips to schedule a meeting. To stop the spread of this viral curriculum vitae, I offer these remedies:

Less is more. The sole purpose of a resume is to get you an interview, period. It's not an autobiography. If you blurt it all out now, why should anyone want to meet you? Rather, think of it as wrapping paper that will make its recipient eager to tear open the package and see what's inside. Once you've accomplished that, take a bow and start working on your interviewing skills.

Report, don't editorialize. Resist the urge to tell me that you're a "highly motivated, results-driven, visionary, world-class entrepreneur." May I decide that for myself, after we've met and I've had time to consider your multitude of accomplishments? Save the adjectives for a topic other than you. This might be hard, I know, but it will be far more meaningful if I conclude that you're a "seasoned, savvy professional with a distinguished career" than if you announce it beforehand and I have to hunt for evidence to support your claim. Give people credit for having a clue and they may just return the compliment.

Control your audience's eye movements and you control the audience. This ancient wisdom comes from Alfred Hitchcock and I urge you to learn from the master. Get your reader on a short leash with a choke-chain. Oh, did someone tell you those horrid little bullets would make it easier to scan your resume? That's exactly why you don't want to use them.

Shameless self-promotions, garish buzzwords and inventive graphics are as image-positive as a polyester leisure suit . . . and about as likely to get you a date. Avoid gimmicks aimed at luring the window shopper inside. If you want to provide a quick and dirty overview for that Attention Deficit Disorder reader in your life, write a brief, dignified paragraph and call it 'Expertise' or 'Summary.' Put it at the top of the page and get out of there.

Just the facts, ma'am. Write the way Jack Webb spoke on *Dragnet*. Simple, direct statements in government-style, gray flannel prose. No lying, no embellishing. Say what you were genuinely responsible for and don't merely feature 'highlights' or 'achievements.' Again, no bullets; they resemble advertising copy. (Think how your filter kicks in when you see media hype. The same goes for hiring managers and recruiters.) So let it look and sound like . . . well, information. Leave out the poetry, together with any other unnecessary words, including articles and pronouns, and write in clear, journalist declarations that begin with verbs ("Woke up. Got out of bed. Dragged a comb . . . "). The number of pages doesn't matter; substance does. Tell your story and be done with it.

Keep it real. If you're a dermatologist in Buffalo who wants a job pitching for the Yankees, you'll need a wicked slider because even the best resume won't help. And no, you can't break down 10 years of accounting experience into core competencies and demonstrate how qualified you are to become the next CFO of Google, either. By all means say what you've done, but if the dots between that and what you'd like to do can't be connected, the resume isn't to blame. Putting your fantasy on paper won't make it come true. Ask yourself honestly, "Can I get there from here?"

Leave your money in the bank. Don't hire a resume writer. Not for $100 and certainly not for $10,000. It's a waste of money. Hire a seventh-grade English teacher to help with your composition, if you need it, but not a pro. Although often well-intentioned and fiercely proud of their so-called credentials, very few professional resume writers have significant, direct experience actually placing executives in corporate functions. While you may be impressed by their aesthetic standards, they simply do not have skin in the game.

Follow the leader. Charles Montgomery Burns (Homer Simpson's boss on *The Simpsons*), arguably the most successful executive of both this century and last, has generously made his opus available to the world. Email me if you would like a copy.

12

ARE YOU GUILTY OF ADJECTIVE ABUSE?

Oh, hello. Didn't see you standing there. Just been reading your resume. Say, are you *really* a 'hands-on' executive? Would your administrative assistant be willing to go on the record with that? And what's the opposite of 'results-driven,' anyway? Results-averse? Results-agnostic? Process-obsessed?

Naturally I don't pretend to know *everything* about resumes – I only see a few hundred each day – but I know what I don't like. In my forthcoming book, *Less Is More: Uncensored Tales of Corporate Endangerment*, I wisely point out that . . . well, that less is more. And vice versa.

As an example, if you begin your summary by claiming to be a "seasoned, savvy professional with a distinguished career," there's nothing left for me to do but hand over my wife and kids. Seriously, good luck with them. (And could I possibly borrow $5,000?) Before I forget to ask, did your last employer sign off on you being a "visionary, world-class entrepreneur," or did you kind of decide that on your own? What would *she* say about you? That the thesaurus called and they want their synonyms back?

The same goes for cover letters. Didn't you hear? The whole world suddenly has a bad case of ADD. Yup, it's official. Attention spans are down to about two or three seconds. (Not me, of course, but everyone else.) It's all, "What have you got? What can you do for me? How many followers do you have on Twitter? Great, well I gotta bounce." You're in the future now. Wake up!

Here's an actual, unedited excerpt from one of my favorite cover letters:

> Twenty four (24) months later, after having done what I had always opted to accomplish and had dreamt to realize, i.e. ride my Harley Davidson, teach, hike and paint; a kind of ennui started to crawl all over me. I began to feel a little melancholy and earnestly yearn for the days when quotidian nonetheless grueling challenges were posed to me and interminable dynamic strategy formulation as well as decision making processes were factually a way of life, a kind of a circadian routine!

Here's another – the preferred method – reproduced in full:

> Attached is my resume. It's my hope that I will bring value to one of your clients.

I rest my case.

Let's stick to the facts, shall we? No lying, no embellishing. Say what you were genuinely responsible for and don't merely feature highlights or achievements. Let it look and sound like, um, *information*. Leave out the poetry, along with any other unnecessary words including articles and pronouns, and write in clear, journalist declarations that begin with verbs. The number of pages doesn't matter; substance does. Tell your story and leave the building.

Think how your own filter kicks in when you read media hype. The same goes for hiring managers and recruiters. Let people reach their own conclusions about just how "performance-based and collaborative" you are by allowing them to participate in the assessment process. In business as in love, infatuation rarely results from a hard sell or a soft shoe routine.

13

BUZZWORDS ARE
BUZZ KILLERS

Business is pretty simple at its core. There are, you know, these basic *rules*. Have a product or service the public wants to buy. Treat people the way you like to be treated. Spend less than you earn. Hire employees who are smarter than you. Keep your hands out of the cash register. Don't hit on the receptionist. Are there others? Probably not.

Sadly, a list of corporate action items waits for no man. Business has to keep moving if it wants to look sharp, and often that's accompanied by a fresh outbreak of buzzwords.

We've all seen it. Principle-centered leaders will go the extra mile, drilling down to the potential synergies between customer needs and brand touchpoints. While this strategy empowers a nimble few to ramp up, stay ahead of the curve and validate best practices within their networks, it also wrongsizes scalable mindshare due to the sheer volume of mission-critical heavy lifting. Not to mention the blocking and tackling. Correct me if I'm wrong – but at the end of the day, it's like herding cats!

Did you have difficulty following that? Good. Now let's get back *inside* the box for a moment.

Here's the rub: Corporations and their shareholders have come to expect positive new developments – often called *results* – to measure financial growth. From nothing more than a casual glance at this formula, the deeper human condition becomes glaringly evident.

Do you see where this is headed? Let's spell it out: Long-term survival depends on constantly changing partners and having as many successive conquests as possible – precisely as factions of us have been attempting to rationalize for years. Believe me, it's a lot of hard work. And then we go someplace nice for lunch.

So success in business is defined by growth and change. It's not that complicated, really, yet the contribution of each era quickly defaults to the jargon it creates, the verbal illusion that we're the ones who will finally cut the crap and revolutionize the economy. The old lexicon would serve admirably if once in a while someone had a new idea or two. If not, maybe bandaging old ideas with new words will suffice.

Imagine you just wrapped up that expensive Harvard MBA and wangled an interview with the marketing department at General Mills. You tell them *what*, exactly? That if they hire you, Cheerios will continue to be a top consumer brand? No, that won't do it. You're going to need *advanced terminology*.

Try this: "As we initiate pushback on the paradigm shift and gain traction – you know, actionable leverage – by examining gap analysis data on the more seamless core competencies at our centers of excellence, it's possible to take this to the next level of penetration without having to circle back on predictable low-hanging fruit. In other words, we can bring value-add to the table *and* capture a win-win solution so long as we stay on the same page and keep everyone in the loop regarding margin factor learnings for deliverables. That's our takeaway, net-net."

Much better.

How will you demonstrate your value to the world of commerce? If you're up to the challenge, you'll be forced to innovate . . . painful as that sounds. And for those moments when creativity fails – as it often does – always bring along a change of idioms to cover your nakedness.

14

A PICTURE TELLS A THOUSAND WORDS

Throughout my career I've prided myself on being a champion of clear, unambiguous communication. No straddling the fence for me. Intelligent life takes a stand. So let's cut to the chase on this topic. Should you display your photo on LinkedIn? The answer is "Maybe."

Common wisdom for the last hundred or so years has been to keep your photo and your credentials completely separate. Good advice, especially if you're the woman who once sent me a portrait of herself sprawled over the top of a grand piano like a torch singer. (She either sold pianos or was an insurance actuary. Whatever. The point is I still remember the picture, but not her resume.)

In the age of social media, however, the rules have become a bit more plastic. People who post a no-nonsense, kick-ass business profile may think it's a good idea to accompany it with a shot of themselves in front of a fireplace next to the family Basset Hound. Occasionally you'll see people at leisure, possibly out among nature, or holding a goblet brimming with something full-bodied while their red eyes flicker demonically. Your next VP of Marketing? I don't think so.

So what are the guidelines? Hmmm . . . let's think. First, tell me why you've included this particular image. Because you like that outfit from your sister's wedding? Huh. I can see it must have been a nice affair. Oh, is that your favorite recliner? Well, you look really comfortable in it.

Sure you want a new job? *Law and Order* is coming on in just a few minutes.

Movie producer Robert Evans has said that if he wears a new tie to a dinner party, he can tolerate one compliment – maybe two. When a third person tells him what a nice tie he's wearing, he takes it off. "The tie is supposed to make *me* look good," he says. "Not the other way around."

The same goes for your mug. Can we see your face clearly? Is it strictly business? Was the photo professionally done? Does it improve on your qualifications? Finally, are you attractive enough to be judged on looks alone? Because that's what you're inviting people to do. And you can't have it both ways – hoping to add cachet, but claiming discrimination if you wind up getting rejected before the first date.

If it's a solid asset, great. Use it, as long as you're absolutely certain that it projects the soul of professionalism. But keep in mind you may be dismissed from consideration – regardless of your credentials, which quite possibly will never be examined – because you're bald, overweight, too young, too old, wearing the wrong suit . . . or, cruelest and most unreasonable of all, too beautiful for your own good.

15

THE NEXT BAD THING

Forget about Ebola. What's really hurting the economy right now is an epidemic of self-esteem.

You've seen the symptoms: Head held high. Confident smile. Pathological sense of well-being in the face of personal and professional disaster. Like Ebola, it appears to spread by human carriers: Corporate trainers. Personal coaches. Employee assistance counselors. And it's lethal to the bottom line.

I should have seen this coming. Murmurs of self-esteem were heard as far back as the early eighties, but I honestly thought it was a marketing gimmick conjured up by some ambitious mental health workers. As a capitalist, I applaud that kind of enterprise and drive. On the other hand, it alarms me now to discover that anxiety, conflict and despair are being routinely labeled as negative conditions for many individuals. No wonder the market's in such a mess. What's the *matter* with everybody?

Call me jaded, but I like working with people who know how to feel bad about themselves, folks who have the decency to wallow in shame when they've squandered someone else's money. I'd much rather do business with a person who's mastered the art of self-flagellation. It saves wear and tear on my own whip.

The process by which self-approval became the Holy Grail for modern civilization is not exactly clear. Somewhere along the way we adopted smugness as a symbol of affluence. Yet we know perfectly well that misery and squalor have always been the springboards to real accomplishment. Indeed, men and women of singular achievement are often recognized by the traumas, insecurities and bad complexions that gave birth to their larger-than-life vision.

Imagine if Napoleon had told himself that it was okay to feel a bit needy at times, and never mind all that stuff about conquering Europe. Suppose Madame Curie had been more comfortable with her body image or if Steven Spielberg had declared his career a success after directing that memorable episode of *Marcus Welby, MD*. Starting to feel a bit like Canada, eh?

By now, no one old enough to read has missed the latest studies dealing with American school children and self-esteem. You know the report – where the kids with the lowest test scores felt the best about themselves and also had the most fun on dates. Why would this surprise anyone who can still remember high school?

Conflict avoidance, risk-aversion, anger management . . . that stuff makes me furious. Okay, everyone's bummed out right now. So what? Confrontation is good for you. Spasms of jealousy alone used to be enough to fuel an entire generation's success. (Those crazy Soviets and their space program – where are they today?) But what was once the gas pedal of progress – basic humiliation, for example – has now become the emergency brake.

Please recall it was suffering and persecution that gave birth to our freedom from King George's tyranny. Let's examine what feeling rotten has done for us as a nation since then. It took us out of the Great Depression. It made us the largest world power. And it's kept *Saturday Night Live* on the air for 40 seasons. Honestly, would you rather be watching reruns of Benny Hill?

Statistics aside, the evidence is overwhelming. Take a confident self-image to its logical conclusion and you have the hubris of a Wall Street CEO. Pure narcissism – the gold standard for what we now refer to as emotional health – combined with a breezy sense of entitlement is the kind of 'feel good now' thinking that begs Sarbanes-Oxley and similar legislation to protect investors from executive greed. On the low end of the scale, these corporate cyborgs are gifted when it comes to making excuses for their behavior. On the high end, why should they need to justify anything to *you?*

Choosing a sample group strictly at random, my staff would do well to spend less time thinking about work-life balance and more time identifying with Sisyphus, that unsung and sadly overlooked hero of Greek mythology. Simply put, why would anyone want to go on vacation when they could stay here with me and be miserable? There's backbreaking work to be done! And what makes you think you've *earned* a vacation, anyway? I mean, besides the employee handbook.

Ultimately, good commerce is built on bad feelings. If I'm OK and you're OK, we don't have much reason to transact, do we? It takes more than a warm smile for someone to turn over cold cash in exchange for products or services. It takes fear. Or greed. Or envy. Or one of those other dark urges we're no longer allowed to discuss.

Of course, you can't really buy happiness. And that's fine. Otherwise there'd be no such thing as repeat business. I mean, we all *say* our goal is customer satisfaction. But satisfied customers don't need you anymore, do they? Restaurants don't stay in business because they satisfy your appetite. They stay in business because, sooner or later, you're going to be hungry again.

So overcome that desire to embrace your limitations. Get in touch with your basic inadequacy. And let's get back to loathing ourselves . . . something we can all feel proud of.

16

IF PEYTON MANNING IS OLD, THEN SO ARE WE

A few years ago I was checking references on a Silicon Valley exec, my client's top choice for a Chief Technology Officer search we'd been doing. It was a pivotal role: tough, competitive industry; Fortune 500 company; fast-paced global blah blah blah . . . in short, the big leagues. And while it's illegal to ask questions about age or even hint that someone might be too old for a given job (funny that we have no problem telling people they're too *young*), I don't think I can get in any trouble now by mentioning that this candidate happened to be well into his 60's. The client and I both thought he was a terrific catch and his age was never discussed. Just the same, I needed specific information from the references – and had no option but to get it sideways. So I used the usual euphemisms, asking about his "bandwidth" and "energy level" and "stamina" and "ability to withstand constant pressure."

I was talking with the last reference on my list – an important one – when he paused and said in his heavy Mandarin accent, "I understand what you are asking and I will tell you. The answer is that *The Force is very strong in him*." (I'm pretty sure that if I hadn't dropped the phone at that point, I would have heard him call me "grasshopper.") In the end, our candidate was offered the position, accepted . . . and performed brilliantly. No surprise, really.

If you're a baby-boomer executive who's recently landed on the ripe side of 50, there's probably less to worry about than there was a generation ago. Except for the economy, of course. Not that you don't have to keep an eye out for a million young Turks who want to eat your lunch – certain things never change. (Free advice: Stay in shape.) But if the current trend in CEO hiring is any evidence, boards of directors have become hugely risk-averse and appear to be more than willing than ever to sacrifice youthful edge and velocity for a few gray hairs.

One thing that may require some adjustment, though, is that the stakes are measurably higher. It hurts much more now when you get sacked. As we often see in professional sports, being too indispensable can wind up feeling like a demotion. If you're not a savior, you're a bum, a has-been. (Isn't that why we say "washed-up," by the way . . . because our player has left the field and gone to the showers?)

Getting older? Don't wait until you're at the top of your game to play like you mean it. (It won't happen unless you make it happen. We only recognize the peak accomplishments in retrospect.) Keep moving, stay warm. Protect your bad ankle and try to avoid helmets to the chin. Sure, you're fragile. C'mon, you're *old!* And yes, it's a lot tougher to pick yourself up after you've been knocked on your ass. But forget about how you look, wipe your nose and find your way back into the huddle. There is no uphill or downhill anymore. There's just being in the game. And hoping that The Force stays with you.

If you ever imagined that you might exit this world with your dignity more or less intact, consider the illustrious Peyton Manning: winning by the occasional miracle, but still losing one piece at a time. It has to be a metaphor for life.

17

ARE YOU CARRYING YOUNG GUY BAGGAGE?

Of all the various ways to differentiate your personal brand – the list goes on and on – here's one profile you may want to avoid: Young Guy Baggage.

Years ago I was speaking to a client about a member of his team. "Steve's a solid performer," the client said, "but he has a fair amount of *young guy baggage*." I admitted that I had never heard the term. Without skipping a beat, he recited, "You know . . . defensive, insecure, always worried about how he looks. Tends to personalize everything."

You just thought of someone who exactly fits that description, didn't you?

By now you've probably figured out that your boss wants you worrying about *her* problems, not yours. Your value will be in rough proportion to your ability to forget personal needs, including concerns of how others perceive you, and focus on the goals of the team. The internal equity you build – indeed, your credibility itself – relies to a significant degree on the knack for recognizing that it's seldom, if ever, about you.

Here's a simple test to see whether you may have one or more latent symptoms. Imagine that I'm your boss. Suppose you ask me a direct question and I give you an evasive response. Is it because I've decided you're not *worthy* to know the answer, or because answering you directly might compromise *me?*

Haven't you found that the more you ask for approval, the more it eludes you? Try to remember that others are focused almost exclusively on their own interests. If you learn to think and feel big-picture, you'll have every strategic advantage. Do you wish you had said something slightly different at that meeting? Chances are no one remembers. They're all on to the next thing. You need to move on, too.

Frustrated with trying to win respect, you may fall into another subtle though predictable trap: You believe you've accomplished the ultimate by not caring what people think about you, but you're still stuck . . . because you want them to know emphatically *how much* you don't care. Gotcha.

If you're asking: Okay, once I drop that whole constellation of neurotic thoughts and behaviors, what do I replace it with? The answer may be to create a 'To Do' list for yourself that looks something like this:

1. Let people underestimate your abilities.

2. Vastly exceed their expectations.

3. Get promoted and enjoy the last laugh.

18

TOXIC RELATIONSHIPS AT WORK

Father Damien Karras: "I think it might be helpful if I gave you some background on the different personalities Regan has manifested. So far, I'd say there seem to be three. She's convinced . . ."

Father Merrin: "There is only one."

The Exorcist

There is no panoply quite so dazzling as the list of unsavory characters you'll encounter at the office. At times it reads like the latest edition of *Diagnostic and Statistical Manual of Mental Disorders*. Or maybe Dante's *Inferno*. How many toxic profiles can you spot from past or current workplaces?

Everyone will recognize the depressive, the abusive, the narcissist, the passive-aggressive and the anal-retentive. But there are more subtle categories, too: projector, cynic, blamer, co-dependent, exhibitionist, martyr, disingenuous, repressed. One symptom will often mask another. Bullies, as we know, are basically insecure. Grandiose personalities may suffer from Imposter Syndrome and the compulsively competitive are just plain annoying.

Factor in a myriad of branches and tributaries (vicious gossip, false friend, shameless user, suck-up . . . the variations go on and on) and soon you'll need to take a power nap. Where do all these unstable people come from, anyway? Did the postal service stop hiring?

Then there are the seemingly infinite patterns of neurotic behavior resulting from – and in turn perpetuating – the underlying conditions found in closed systems, where resistance to change is fundamental. Unspoken beliefs, rules and expectations are always a trap in such environments. Blind obedience bottled as 'teamwork' or 'cooperation' is equally destructive. Enmeshment and pressure to conform 'no matter what' stifle the creative potential of individuals and groups. Speed limits are strictly enforced.

But identifying, cataloguing and analyzing every type of aberration is a task for mental health professionals. So if that's not your career, go ahead and take the day off. It's far more practical – and way easier for me – to lump them all into one neat little radioactive basket: Emotional Neediness (EN).

Think of EN as a form of attention deficit. Attention *deprivation*, really, Godzilla-style. Not enough of the right kind of attention elsewhere in life and now the pain has migrated here. People, like Japanese movie monsters, will attempt every conceivable strategy to compensate those missing nutrients. What's for lunch? Marketing? Mmmmmm . . . they taste a bit like chicken.

It takes two distinct types of EN to make a lethal cocktail: yours and the other person's. Through simple awareness of your own unresolved issues, you can avoid having to re-enact with co-workers scenes from an imperfect past. When there's a conflict, be clear about what's your responsibility and what isn't. Quit trying to fix people; don't even tell them what their problem is. The exact cause of the neediness is irrelevant, no matter whose it is. What matters is that you learn how to dodge the bullets of someone else's unhappy childhood or marriage by declining a part in their Passion Play.

Tolstoy began his novel *Anna Karenina* by announcing, "Happy families are all alike; every unhappy family is unhappy in its own way." Companies are surely as complex and chaotic as families. And managers can appear, at the most inconvenient times especially, as clueless as sitcom dads. It's a blurry line between life and work.

I'll be the first to admit that I'm not immune. For seven and a half years I was in what could only be described as a dysfunctional relationship. Whenever I walked in the door, it was always, "Do you realize what time it is? Where have you been? Who were you with? You never tell me anything! We're not communicating!" So I finally had to let my assistant go. The new one is much better, but she thinks I don't respect her boundaries. At least that's what her diary says.

We all carry our parents around inside us, don't we? Whether living or not, they're alive in our thoughts and feelings. They gave us life and remain primary forces that animate and sustain us throughout our existence, like respiration and circulation. Much of it was enriching and some of it, no doubt, was limiting. Either way, by taking stock of personal baggage you'll be able to circumnavigate a thousand and one snares that could otherwise impede your professional journey. And by recalling that toxic behavior in yourself and others comes from a *single source*, you can move on to more important things.

My editor likes me to offer concrete advice, so here it is: Going to the office? Leave Mom and Dad at home.

19

PASSIVE-AGGRESSIVE? MOI?

So you think you have what it takes to be passive-aggressive. Did you say "Yes"? Do you really mean "Maybe"? Do you resent the directness of the question? Wondering what gives me the right to ask? If so, you may be embarking on one of the most demanding – and emotionally rewarding – adventures of your life.

The path of the true passive-aggressive is not for everyone. Sadly, there is no shortage of impostors. Forget the off-key humming in the next cubicle or the driver who pretends not to notice when you try to merge into his lane. Strictly amateur hour. Likewise the procrastinator, the indolent, the weak-willed – none should be confused with the genuine article. It takes guts and it takes brains. This is about getting what you want without ever having to admit that you want it.

Avoiding confrontation and resisting change require a rare spark, similar to courage but without the moral foundation. Unable to make up your mind? Unwilling to distinguish between worthy and unworthy? These are not flaws, my friend. They're core competencies. Embrace them! Such valuable talents must be harnessed, molded and sharpened into potential weapons against those you perceive as threatening.

Basic to your world view, of course, is the conviction that nobody has the right to know how you actually feel. Thoughts are private, emotions sacred. *Sanctum sanctorum*. And no, it's not up for discussion. You can stay the course only if you have a stomach for battle. We're talking survival skills here. Your family, your job – indeed, your very selfhood – is at stake.

Try this simple test. Say you run marketing for a Fortune 500 company which recently acquired a start-up, one that had begun to nibble at your revenue base. As it turns out, their top marketing exec has a much better resume than yours, but since you're on the buy side of the deal, the CEO has decided to let you share the position of Chief Marketing Officer with the other guy. Co-CMO, that's your new title.

When your colleague shows up for his first day of work, do you:

A. Make it clear to him that you're in charge because your company bought his.

B. Openly defer to his greater expertise and tell him you'll have much to learn.

C. Leave an anonymous note for Legal and Human Resources saying that he's been sexually harassing everyone on your floor.

Okay, that was easy. The correct answer is B . . . and C.

Now try this. You've been working for six months on a customer segmentation analysis which is critical to your next product release, and it's nearly done.

Do you:

A. Complete the project as quickly and quietly as possible and present the data at the next senior staff meeting.

B. Ask your partner to help add the finishing touches and present it together.

C. Use your executive washroom key to destroy the paint job on his BMW.

A bit trickier, right? Again, B *and* C. Is the profile coming into focus?

Here's an extra credit problem for overachievers. Suppose you've been recruited by a competitor for a bigger role with more status and tons of cash. Do you:

A. Tell the CEO that the team arrangement has been a disaster and that your departure was long overdue.

B. Tell the CEO that you hate to say goodbye, but it's always been your family's dream to live in Akron.

C. Tell the CEO basically nothing, but a week after you leave, send a letter explaining that your former colleague's behavior created a hostile work environment and that they'll both be hearing from your attorney.

Don't have to give you the answers anymore, do I? Congratulations, you plucky grad! Now go out and spin something wild and surreptitious with that freshly hatched power of yours. Better hang on tight, because the challenges will start multiplying. React too quickly and you run the risk of exposure. Hesitate too long and you might forfeit the prize to a less qualified adversary. And believe me, they're out there . . . ready to take away every shred of self-determination you've worked so hard to conceal.

There's no need to wait for inspiration. You can do this today, in the office or at leisure, without any rationale at all. Just remember that no commitment is binding – *ever* – other than the commitment to stay in control. And the best practice, the way to really build up calluses, is to say nothing of substance when asked. They'll get the message eventually, after it's too late. Then we'll see who's sorry for not asking you:

A. Sooner

B. More nicely

C. On bended knee

D. All of the above

20

THE DRAMA OF BEING DISCOVERED

In case you haven't already seen through the mask and pegged me as a sentimental slob, I'd like to acknowledge one of the magical moments in business. (No, it's not when those options backdating charges are dropped due to insufficient evidence.) This luminous event happens when you meet a person who looks a thousand miles beyond your resume and has some kind of glimpse into what you might become. A star is born!

Ever wonder how superstars become superstars? There's an old Hollywood saying that nobody knows anything. Or do they? William Wilkerson, publisher of *The Hollywood Reporter*, spotted 16 year-old Lana Turner sipping a Coke at the Top Hat Café on Sunset Boulevard one afternoon when she was supposed to be in typing class. He introduced her to Zeppo Marx, the agent, and the rest is show biz. True, she did look great in a sweater – and maybe Wilkerson would never have noticed her without that salient fact. But let's not ruin the story by analyzing it.

We now know beyond any reasonable doubt that much of what we were taught about how to succeed in life is goofy, wrong-headed, or just plain false. As Daniel Pink points out in his brilliant illustrated career manual, *The Adventures of Johnny Bunko:* "There is no plan."

Education? Please consider Bill Gates, Steve Jobs, Michael Dell, Ted Waitt and Larry Ellison, all of whom, if I'm not mistaken, bailed out of college and yet managed to transform the modern world.

Loyalty – the quaint belief that if you serve one master for years on end (like in the Bible), prosperity will take care of itself – died a swift and merciless death not long after Noah's flood.

Pedigree works well enough if you're in line to inherit millions. But if you need to actually earn a living, don't expect even the most glorious family tree to bear any fruit.

Prestige is always an intoxicating brew. When you have a few hours to spare, I'd be thrilled to narrate stories from the golden era of IBM. What's that? You'd rather listen to Nancy Pelosi talk about healthcare reform? What-*ever*.

You can pretty much forget professional apprenticeships, too. Why would anyone be willing to invest a ton of time and energy these days developing a young person who's not likely to hang around? Or worse, might hang around just long enough to walk off with the mentor's client list.

What's more likely to occur is that somewhere along the line, your boss gets stuck. He's up against a wall and has tried everything he knows: blaming his predecessor, blaming the IT department, blaming marketing. Nothing works, and chances are he didn't get where he is today by solving problems himself. Where will he turn for a solution?

Here is where you come in, and why you have nothing to lose and everything to gain. Offer to solve the problem. Write up a plan. Tell the boss what resources you need to do it. Make it clear that he'll get all the credit. If you succeed — by some wondrous stroke of karma — you've 'made your bones' and can flog that triumph for many years to come. Not to mention being your boss' number one secret weapon for as long as you breathe. Should you fail, there are two redeeming features. First, you get an honorable mention for failing spectacularly. (Pink refers to these as "excellent mistakes.") Second, your contract has just been extended with a valuable new title: Scapegoat.

This may not sound exactly like the mystical awakening described earlier. There may be no prophetic visions, shining auras, celestial music or weeping angels. Maybe your boss is basically unimaginative and self-absorbed. Maybe he was so desperate he would've tried anything. Or maybe he just liked your perfume. Either way, it's the closest thing I've seen to childbirth.

21

TELLING YOUR BOSS THE TRUTH

A recent study of CEOs revealed that the number one side effect of the job – in addition to fear of losing the corporate jet – is a growing sense of isolation. No surprise, really. If you were constantly surrounded by people whose paychecks you signed, who would *you* turn to for unvarnished feedback and data that hadn't been fluffed?

In olden times a king would be flanked by his courtiers, the usual obsequious parasites and leering, fork-tongued politicians. (I know that actually sounds pretty cool, but believe me, it gets tiresome after a while.) Only one individual was authorized to deliver what are now called difficult messages, and that was the Court Jester, or, as he was more affectionately known, Fool.

Fool had a special template for delivering unflattering memos. They were encrypted through verse, ditty and humorous quips. So if the king had toilet paper (or the medieval, metaphorical equivalent of such) stuck to his royal footwear, Fool would telegraph that critical information to His Highness as he entertained him. No one else had impunity to address the throne with such frankness, including those of superior status. Anyone who dared to would have met the dungeon . . . or worse.

To a large degree management consultants have filled that role in contemporary business, assuming they are smart and colorful enough to get away with it. Somewhere in the past decade, though, consultants became as salesman-like as the rest of the boss's entourage. And a CEO who can no longer rely on outsiders for a dose of tough reality could easily misplace his compass and map.

Here's an opportunity for an energetic up-and-comer, maybe a younger person who doesn't have the universe to lose: Be the person your boss trusts. Earn that trust by saying the hard thing, the thing that nobody else has the insight or courage to say. Let your boss feel that she's received something more valuable than a token pledge of loyalty.

It's true, bosses can be fragile. And you can probably guess that the bigger the ego, the more delicacy is required. But tact doesn't mean avoidance of difficult messages. It means expressing your ideas in a caring, diplomatic fashion. You'd want someone to tell you if you had ketchup on your tie, wouldn't you?

So consider letting the emperor know when he's not wearing any clothes. Gently and privately, of course. You may just find that a lowly member of the court is the obvious choice to be his most trusted advisor.

22

DISCRETION IS THE BETTER PART OF VALOR

Though it should seem obvious, like "don't stick your hand in the garbage disposal while it's running," there's a blinking light on the console telling me to make another public service announcement. Hard to imagine, but somebody must have forgotten somewhere. So here's your formal reminder, pal . . . and don't let it happen again.

People you know and people you don't know don't want to hear what's the matter with them. Especially from you. Sorry, but that's just how it is. It's not that they don't appreciate your wisdom and keen insight. They do! But they have other things to worry about at the moment. Think back. Did it ever work in the past? Has anyone in recent memory told you, "Thanks for pointing out what a jerk I am! I'm so pleased you spoke up!"? Probably not.

Co-workers, friends, family members and casual acquaintances, specifically, have long memories when it comes to you saying negative things about them. You know this, so why deny it? You are free to deny any gossip or slander that's been attributed to your name, naturally. But when you tell someone straight out what you think his or her problem is, even in that delightful, well-intentioned way you have, your cover is blown. Game over.

Here's the crazy part: People want you to figure out how they see themselves – on a good day – and confirm it for them. Period. It's also essential that you *approve*. They hope that you'll notice and validate their unique identity, and buy into the image they have, or would like to have, of themselves as heroes in their own stories. (Don't laugh. You want it, too.)

Continue to validate someone's fondest self-image – punch that ticket for him – and he'll be your ally for life. Doesn't that amount to cheap flattery? No, most emphatically not . . . unless you're faking. Which I don't recommend, because you'll eventually get caught. Insincerity is much more difficult than it sounds; doing it well takes years of dedicated practice.

Oh, but now you say, "Mr. Mark Jaffe of mysterious origin and sketchy locale, you are clearly one confused dude! Didn't you just recommend that by telling your boss the truth, an employee builds credibility and trust?" Well, you are absolutely right, my perceptive reader. I did say that. (Please keep those cards and letters coming.)

First, that only works with a direct or dotted-line superior. If you try pulling it on a peer or a subordinate, or worse, jump levels and go above your boss' head, it'll backfire. Big time. Providing such specialized service at critical moments is a professional courtesy, on par with a fastidious butler who ensures that his master's coat is lint-free. (Think Bruce Wayne's Alfred.) You must stay in character and remain steadfastly loyal. Second, it's not a summary – ever – or a general diagnosis of what you think is 'wrong' with the person. It's a random flash in time, a mere anecdote. Certainly nothing that *defines*.

For more on how to deal effectively with the powerful and the super rich, read my forthcoming book, *Less Is More: It Usually Costs Nothing to Say Nothing*. (I can neither confirm nor deny that Beyoncé will be appearing at the book release to demonstrate her friendship, admiration and support. You'll have to wait and see.)

I would hope it's understood that I'm not advising people to withhold their opinions from each other, particularly at work. Because I love a good fistfight. But it can't be personal. Or prescriptive. Which brings us back to our fundamental rule: It costs nothing to say nothing. Most of the time. So when in doubt, try going with that.

23

WHY IS IT SO HARD TO SAY "I DON'T KNOW"?

Any executive recruiter worth his salt will recognize when a candidate is fudging the truth. Not because we're clairvoyant or have special techniques for monitoring eye movements, body language and respiration. But kind of like people can tell the difference between butter and margarine in, say, a croissant. You can just *taste* it – and the flavor doesn't lie. (Let's see . . . salt, fudge, butter, margarine, croissants. Guess that pretty much covers the basic food groups.) When you try to bluff your way through a response, even a smidgen, it's ridiculously obvious. Ask a homicide detective if you don't believe me.

As products and services have become increasingly commoditized in recent years, there has been endless talk about how to differentiate our business offerings. While everyone agrees that competing primarily on price is the *lowest* common denominator, the path leading to unique and lasting value – let alone graceful execution – is a steep one for most of us to climb. In other words, substance is no longer enough. If you hope to survive, you'll need to come up with some sexy 'extras.'

Whether you represent an old-line brand that's trying to hold on to your customers or a renegade trying to gain traction, a white-shoe firm that would like to continue feeling smug or a maverick out to change the rules, the simplest and most elegant way to stand above the crowd will always be *through the virtue of your actions*. Not sincerity and warm intentions, nor facile words and flattery, but straightforward honesty and best-effort delivery. It means taking individual responsibility, making good on promises, not exaggerating, always having your mouth and your heart in perfect agreement.

None of this is easy. (If it were, everyone would do it and we'd be back to same problem of how to distinguish premium from regular.) It takes serious commitment. And of all the strands that comprise our human integrity molecule, I suspect the hardest one to acquire is the ability to say, "I don't know."

Here's how it usually goes: You're interviewing with a manager and it's important for her to understand exactly where your relevant experience begins and ends. If she does her job right, the discussion will ultimately reach the borders of your personal 'known' and cross over into the wilderness of your 'unknown.' That's just effective interviewing, since she needs to gauge the limits and shape of your skill set.

How will you handle that inevitable moment when it occurs? You've been talking confidently for 20 minutes about been-there-done-that accomplishments, enjoying the glow of being on top of your game. You answer, "Yes, yes and yes again" to question after question, but now she's asking you about stuff that's . . . well, *not you*.

This is a painful anti-climax for many. After soaring in the clouds with a steady tailwind, the left engine suddenly starts to cough and sputter. Then you lose both props and go into a nosedive.

You'll do almost anything to avoid it — you don't want to disappoint — and yet you hear yourself meekly whisper, "Nope, haven't done that. Not sure." And then the worst: "I don't know."

Similar to falling in a dream, right? Is it really so bad? You're still alive; chances are you haven't even wet your pants. So why do our pathetic little egos consistently recoil in horror from that innocent statement of fact?

The answer is: *I don't know.* (I just don't, sorry. Ask a philosopher, maybe. If he's honest, he'll probably tell you that he doesn't know, either.) What I do know is that if you say it often enough and without shame, you will forever establish your reputation as a straight shooter and a modest, authentic person who is not embarrassed to be merely human. People will remember you. You'll have credibility, an insurance policy on everything you *do* know and say. Because when you admit to not knowing, your knowing has far greater value.

Now, back to the interview. Want to turn a negative into a positive? Instead of saying, "No, I've never done that" and feeling miserably sullen afterwards, try this: "You know, I haven't had the opportunity to do that before, but always wished I could learn. Would I be able to *here?*"

24

YOU'RE SO VAIN

It's been fascinating to watch from my front-row seat as an executive recruiter the ever-changing fashions for business etiquette. Letitia Baldrige, a personal favorite of mine, implies that the rules of professional conduct are carved on hefty stone tablets. But many of the principles once considered timeless were, for an anxious period, regarded as merely quaint. Sort of like Brooks Brothers suits.

Please don't misunderstand. I never recommended that all 'new economy' executives be rounded up and herded into finishing schools. And I certainly enjoy breaking dishes as much as the next guy. There does seem to be a mysterious relationship, however, between good times and bad manners. More to the point: Aren't you glad people have their humility back, even if the new 'new economy' really sucks?

By way of illustration, allow me to guide you – forcibly, if necessary – behind the scenes of an *actual executive search*. You'll need a hardhat and a shovel.

During the summer of 2000, the nationwide hiring frenzy approached toxic levels. I had been retained to recruit a general manager for the northeast region of a highly publicized, blue-chip venture startup located in Silicon Valley. Money was no object for the right person . . . within reason.

After rounds of grueling interviews with the leading road-warrior types, my client narrowed in on an executive from a major telecom provider and offered him an irresistible package. The candidate was ready to sign when I issued my standard warning: "Don't accept unless you are absolutely firm in your decision. It has to be a solid gold 'Yes' or nothing."

"Mark," he said, "you haven't read me very well if you're worried about that. My word is my bond."

We met less than a week later in Manhattan to toast the deal. "You might be a little upset," he blurted out immediately. "My employer couldn't afford to lose me right now. I've taken a substantial retention bonus to stay on for another year."

"But your word was your bond," I managed to say. "That was what? Five days ago?"

"Please don't make it worse," he whimpered, his face turning green. "I feel bad enough as it is. They're giving me $600,000 to hang in there." I asked him what he was taking for the pain.

Exactly a year later he contacted me. Now a layoff casualty dripping with good-natured camaraderie, he wanted to know if I "had anything" for him. He could probably hear my choking sounds through the phone when he added, "I also wanted to make sure that you and I are, you know, okay professionally."

This is the part where I really should assume a posture of moral superiority. Don't count on it. I'm not as limber as I used to be.

Is it just my skewed perception, or were egos running completely amok a few short minutes ago? And have you noticed the most recent change? There's still no shortfall of "lie now and we'll deal with it later." But a fundamental shift in attitude has occurred somewhere in our collective conscience, lending business people a not completely unattractive new aura of fallibility.

This transmigration of mood and deportment extends to dress codes, as well. Since no one knows how to repair the market, an increasingly widespread superstition suggests that abolishing casual attire at the office will somehow restore our self-respect and thereby our prosperity. I'd be willing to give it a try if I could only find my Chesterfield coat.

Today, just about everybody returns emails and phone calls. More or less. There may be a slight residue of hubris lingering. Still, mending poorly managed relationships has become top priority. I know several CEOs who have even taken to calling their mothers on a weekly basis.

It wasn't simply about greed, though, was it? That was a different administration. Instead, we saw an economy so fluid, so buoyant that the opportunities seemed boundless, the inexperienced promising and the incompetent trustworthy. Not only did we over-value our assets, but we shaped them in our own worst image. Now, as the flotsam and jetsam clear, we remember that integrity and modesty are not strictly anathema to sound enterprise.

Let's keep an eye on the social graces of those we encounter in business: When professionalism and ethical practices lose their currency again, I bet you'll find the economic recovery is well under way.

25

THE ART OF THE DANCE

We have a pretty terrific system in America: Careers are open to talent. I'm not saying it's a pure meritocracy, but compared to other countries and cultures, we completely rock. Who your parents were, how you grew up, even where you went to school (unless it was Yale, of course) . . . all these factors are secondary to whether or not you can deliver the goods.

Getting through the interview, though, is another story.

At last count, there were just over four million books published on the subject of interviewing for jobs. They tell you how to dress for success, how to sell yourself and how to answer all the tricky questions. Most important, they give you the confidence that only comes with having read a book or two. There's nothing like it.

My grandmother, bless her soul, used to say, "Never raise a child by the book until your child is old enough to read the same book." And therein lies the rub. Assuming you and whoever conducts the interview are using the same script, it's akin to Hollywood magic. But what if the interviewer didn't study his or her lines? What if that person read – gulp – a *different* book?

Let's skip the obvious rules of engagement for a minute. I'm sure you don't need me to warn you about discussing money, politics or your personal history with alien abductions on the first date. Where people have the most difficulty is with the Fred Astaire - Ginger Rogers thing, the dynamic that defines whether you're dancing forward or backward.

Starting with basics, who is the buyer and who the seller in your scenario? If you're out of work, you may very well be stuck in the seller role. Put on your tap shoes. If you've been *recruited* to this interview, then maybe you're the buyer. And maybe not.

Here's how it usually goes: On one side of the desk sits the candidate – you – arms folded across your chest, waiting to hear from the interviewer why you should drop everything and consider moving your family a zillion miles to take this one specific job out of all the possible jobs in the world.

On the other side of the desk sits the CEO or CFO or HR Chief or whomever, arms also folded in judgment. She wants you to be clear that this role is mission critical, essential to the success of the organization, the most important job in the company. So why, of all the possible candidates in the world, should she consider you the best qualified?

It's a standoff.

If you think about it, this really is a flawed model, awkward at best, adversarial at worst. There's simply no agreement about who's Fred Astaire and who's Ginger Rogers. Each of you knows intuitively that there must be some blend of selling and buying in your exchange . . . but in what sequence or proportions? How much self-promotion versus how much scrutiny? What's the routine? Who's on first?

My solution is ridiculously simple. Forget about being a candidate . . . totally. Imagine instead that you're a consultant, and that you've already been paid a non-refundable $20,000 consulting fee to attend this meeting.

How does that change things?

For one, you don't have to worry about selling yourself. No posing, no posturing, no tap dancing of any kind. You're there to be helpful, to identify your client's needs. You simply want to *add value*, to give them their $20,000 worth of empathy and understanding. If you deliver, they're likely to come back for more of your time and expertise.

Now you can sit on the same side of the table, metaphorically speaking, and ask the hard questions. Not as a skeptic, but as a doctor or analyst might do while conducting a thorough exam. You'll want to hear where this organization has been, where it is today and what type of goals its executives would like to achieve. What's the history of this particular role? How did the company come to define it as such? How will its executives recognize top performance and by what method will they calibrate results? The very questions you ask will tell your interviewers volumes about who you are and how you think.

Listen to how they self-diagnose while you make your own private diagnosis. Consider whether your assessment matches theirs. Never mind whether you're the right person for this role. You can think about that later, in the car on the way home.

What will stick with them is that you asked the right questions, paid close attention to the answers and really fathomed what their organization is all about. Now they're hooked.

Just remember: It's not about you; it's all about them. The more you want to be taken seriously as a candidate, the more you should forget that you are one.

26

ASK A STUPID QUESTION . . .

An ambitious young advertising executive called me last week in tears. Between sobs, she managed to report that she'd just been through the most demeaning experience of her career.

"Were you fired?" I asked, radiating sympathy and paternal concern. "Demoted?"

"No," she said. "Worse."

"Sexual harassment?" I said. "Just tell me who it was and I'll lash him with my acid tongue."

"More humiliating," she whispered hoarsely.

"Don't tell me they cut your dental coverage," I said. This was potentially serious stuff.

"No," she said. "I was interviewing for that managing director position in our Sydney office. And I had to meet with the agency's chief recruiting officer in London."

"What happened?" I said. "Was there a problem? Did she make you eat English food? Were there kidneys involved?"

"It's not a joke. She asked . . . she asked . . . "

"C'mon, you can do it. Tell me what she said."

"She asked if I were a breakfast cereal, what kind would I be!"

"Um . . . alright. And what did you say?"

"That's the problem, I froze! I didn't know *what* to say. I just sat there like an idiot with a big dumb grin on my face. It was the worst interview ever!"

"Okay," I admitted. "That is huge. I can't believe you screwed up so badly, particularly with your credentials. Look at it this way: Where do you see yourself in five years – what about in ten – if you can't even answer a simple question? Why should they hire you?"

"You're not making this easier," she whimpered.

"Try to relax," I said reassuringly. "Maybe you'll feel better if you tell me about your worst boss."

Ever notice how every single person you've met throughout your whole life thinks he has a good sense of humor? Good taste in clothes? Believes herself to be a nice person? A good judge of character? A good interviewer? What's up with that?

Ensuring a successful hire is both art and science. Multiple, interrelated factors such as years of relevant experience, proficiency with specific tools, problem-solving ability, capacity for teamwork, motivation, stamina, cultural fit and proprietary company resources are all fundamental.

Oddly, final decisions about a candidate's fit within the organization are often connected to drippy questions like, "What do you most want to be remembered for?"

When I entered the search profession 30 years ago, it had recently become vogue for employers to ask candidates to identify their "biggest weakness" during an interview. Believe it or not, people actually struggled three or four seconds to find the best answer for this until it became apparent to everyone – all at once, it seemed – to say, "I work too hard. I take my job too seriously." Whew.

Then those sneaky hiring managers found another, even more diabolical way to get at the same information. They started asking, "What's a common misperception people have about you?" The idea, of course, is that there are no misperceptions, and if you were naïve enough to walk into such an obvious trap, you sang like a canary. If you were on your toes, you suavely dodged a bullet by saying, "I don't really think people have any misperceptions about me. They unanimously agree that I'm a gifted genius and a selfless humanitarian."

The worst part is that there are no right answers to touchy-feely questions. You can't study, you can't rehearse. Oh yeah . . . that, and the fact that none of this fluff has anything to do with your qualifications. What kind of animal are you? How do you take criticism? Can you work under pressure and deadlines? Are you a Mac or a PC? Did you ever punch an interviewer square in the face?

Sad to say, stupid interview questions haven't gone away – they've just become more numerous and more annoying. While we're on the subject: What *are* your salary expectations, anyway?

27

THE PROBLEM WITH OVER-SELLING YOURSELF

"I don't want to sell anything, buy anything, or process anything as a career. I don't want to sell anything bought or processed, or buy anything sold or processed, or process anything sold, bought, or processed, or repair anything sold, bought, or processed. You know, as a career, I don't want to do that."

Lloyd Dobler (John Cusak) in Say Anything

Are you a bit like Lloyd? Do you hate selling, too? Don't you wish everybody did?

This may be difficult for certain people to hear. Countless thousands – perhaps millions – of serious grownups the world over make a living trying to find new and innovative ways to get you to eat your vegetables. Or whatever. Do you enjoy being on the receiving end of these strategies? No? There is nothing wrong with you if not. Perhaps, like me, you wonder: Is all this huffing and puffing really necessary?

Today I come not to condemn – as is usually the case – but to reassure. If being pitched the virtues of a product, service or relationship by someone dripping with good-natured camaraderie makes you want to set fire to your hair, you're perfectly healthy. And if the thought of spending more than four minutes alone with any living creature whose motto is "Always Be Closing" has you reconsidering your membership in the human race, please know that you are not alone. (I wish I could say that help was on the way, but we're still working on that part.)

Even worse, if possible, than the classic back-slappery of old-school salesmanship is the latest breed of super-sensitive, 'collaborative sales' types. You know who I mean. This is the person who wears the self-righteous grimace of a marriage counselor and tries to gently probe for your centers of pain. "Are you happy with your current ointment? Is it possible that your rash deserves more tender, loving attention?" He wants you to think that he's not really a salesman. He's a trusted advisor! And he's thinking about your problem at this very moment! ("How much did you say you were willing to spend on a global solution for that rash?")

Could it get any worse? You betcha. Welcome to the world of sales karaoke. The popular wisdom *du jour* is for everyone to sell like mad, no matter what your chosen profession. Pull out the stops, reinvent yourself. Since no one knows how, exactly, to survive in this economy, the prescription for some reason has been to sell harder and faster and better and then sell some more.

An allergic reaction to selling does not mean you were damaged at birth. And it shouldn't matter whether you're a terminally shy, Type-B personality, or a flaming extrovert. Type-A people can hate selling, too. Contrary to popular belief, not everyone who is verbal or even aggressive will be a natural with sales. Would you buy something from Rush Limbaugh? Or Andy Dick?

When you launch into a self-promotional episode (the new Tourette Syndrome?) while interviewing, the person on the other side of the desk instinctively takes a few steps back. Hardly anyone likes to be pitched, okay? And when you scream your qualifications into the face of some hapless individual who was unfortunate enough to look at your resume, you run the risk of alienating that reader with every bullet, adjective and buzzword.

So even if the whole world is telling you to put on those tap shoes and peddle your brand, there's no shame in feeling a little revulsion. And if you continue to cringe at the sound of shrill pitchmen, smarmy snake oil salesmen, and shameless hucksters, there's nothing wrong with you. It'll all be better when the recession is over. Trust me.

28

IT'S NOT YOU

There's a new designer cologne on the market, one that's becoming oh-so-fashionable. While advertisements for this product are wonderfully seductive – appealing to our most basic fears – I just can't bring myself to endorse it. The claims are predictably too good to be true: *One scent and potential employers won't be able to resist you.* It's called Desperation® and is now available almost everywhere you look.

Never mind what you've heard about differentiating yourself in this business climate. Bleak as it may be, the solution is not finding more elaborate gimmicks or reaching the perfect pitch of frenzy. Forget the video cover letter, the chocolate chip cookie resume and the Robin Williams interview style. And please curb your impulse to bring the hiring manager an adorable puppy.

There are some basic guidelines for self-advancement even under the worst of conditions. Radiating pure terror is not among them. What is? Be yourself. Do your homework and try to understand what the company needs. Talk about your successes, providing concrete examples. Smile occasionally.

Here are a few more recommendations for professionals who want to make a better first, second, and third impression while weathering an unemployment tsunami:

Try to stay calm. Take a deep breath and relax. Hyperventilating is never pretty, particularly during an interview. Prospective employers want Jason Bourne – not Jason Alexander. Show them you're capable, confident and cool. No sobbing.

Come down off that ledge. Please remember that what's happening is a reflection of the overall economy. It's not a commentary on your specific qualifications. Sometimes stuff just happens . . . and we all get stuffed in the process. Don't take it personally.

Revitalize, don't reinvent. Why is 'reinvent' even a word? Companies need the experience and accomplishments you've earned over time. Leave the instant makeovers for people who have something to hide. Leverage what you already have instead of focusing on what you fear you may lack.

Hold on to your cash. When times get tough, the tough get pitched a bunch of crap. If someone offers to craft you a killer resume, put you in touch with the hidden job market or coach you to become a newer, more marketable you, keep your wallet in its holster. Whether they're asking for $3,000 or $300, it's overpriced. Don't take candy from strangers, either.

Romance trumps selling. Your next boss wants to be enamored, not assaulted. By all means explain, but resist the urge to *exclaim*. Let people reach their own conclusions about just how 'world-class' an employee you are.

Be realistic. Naked ambition is a great thing, especially on reality TV, but baby steps may be more effective at the moment. Besides, starting at the top is overrated. Set your goals at achievable levels.

Give yourself some time. Listening too closely to your inner job clock can get you wound way too tight. Yes, time is of the essence – there's not a minute to waste – but most people underestimate how long it will take to find the right gig. Pace yourself and spare the whip.

Work your contacts, but don't work them over. Chances are you already know the person who will put you on the path to your next salary. Your network is a precious resource and should be treated as such. Now is the time to use it . . . but gently. Ask for a reference, not a job. When you don't put your friends on the spot, they're more inclined to think about ways to help you.

Choose wisely. If Smokey Robinson was recording "Shop Around" today, he'd probably say, "Try to get yourself a bargain, son. Don't be sold on the very first one. Pretty jobs come a dime a dozen. Try to find one that's gonna give you true lovin'." Or something like that. Smokey knows about life. To whatever degree possible, avoid jumping into a situation where you think you'll be unhappy. There's always another choice.

This too shall pass. Despite what you see on the cable networks, we are not living in the End of Days. Yes, it's miserable out there – worse than most of us have ever seen – but at some point it will just be a bad memory. Sooner than you or anyone at CNBC imagines.

Don't put your faith in recruiters. Seriously. We are not the answer to your prayers. Most of us never even answer our phones.

Take another deep breath. Admit it, you're all tensed up again. Deep breath, cleansing breath. And . . . exhale. Once more . . . and exhale.

OK, now you're ready. Check the mirror, buff your shoes and go. You look good.

29

I LIKE-A YOUR FACE AND THAT-SA GOOD ENOUGH FOR ME

Groucho: "Now what about references?"

Chico: "You don't need any reference. I like-a your face and that-sa good enough for me."

The Marx Brothers

As we have discussed earlier, people who conduct interviews tend to think of themselves as pretty shrewd customers. Sadly, nothing could be further from the truth. Mining for tangible experience and arriving at a clear picture of a candidate's past performance is never simple or painless. Even when you take the right tissue and fluid samples and have them properly analyzed, just like on CSI, connecting the dots – projecting those results onto another job at a different company so as to accurately predict success – can put the most accomplished interviewer up against a wall. If it were easy, then everyone would do it all the time, right?

Perhaps the biggest mistake hiring managers make, in very general terms, is to base their decisions on a candidate's personality and presentation: Do I like this person or not? Rather than hunting for tangible evidence of competencies in specific areas, that old reptilian brain kicks in with its evolution-based programming for self-preservation. Is it safe or dangerous to add this person to our group? Who's guarding the offspring? Whom do we eat? No wonder the weaker individual so frequently gets hired.

This comedy of errors will often compound to a ridiculous degree when it comes to reference checks. Rather than looking for relevant insights, we see managers hoping to validate their own perceptions of the candidate; actually leading the witness, as they say in courtroom dramas, by setting up good/bad options in an obvious way. ("Has he demonstrated any aggressive behaviors, particularly during a full moon?")

In response to the standard questions flows a litany of clichés. (How does she handle conflict? In what ways did you see him grow? Describe his management style. What type of boss can you see her working with best?) Oh baby! Lifeless, passive and uninsightful. The reference checker rarely 'drives the car' in any purposeful direction and we're left on the side of the road never learning about the candidate's true abilities. In the end, what we have is the superficial comments of three or four faceless 'others' – just humdrum frozen dinners utterly lacking in color, texture or interpretation. We hear what people say about the candidate, but those comments don't reflect any wisdom or fresh perspective. Everything about this process is run-of-the-mill, as you should expect if references are not asked appropriately meaningful questions. Convenience food at its worst.

We don't realize any conclusions, either. Since there's no scorecard, we don't come away grasping anything about the candidate's limitations or needs. So she's 'big picture.' Therefore what? You say she doesn't react well to abrasive people? Now *that's* a revelation. Everyone knows that mean people suck. It's as if the reference had said, "Sometimes he eats and sometimes he sleeps and sometimes he plays golf." But who *is* he? These observations – if you could even call them that – land on us with a dull thud, and then lay there like a beached mackerel. Is it any surprise that employees who snap and go on murderous rampages are almost always described, after the fact, as having "gotten along well with others?" That's the banal voice-over of references talking.

So what, exactly, are you after when you ask those same tired reference-check questions? How do you get your witness to deliver the goods? And if you don't know the reference personally – her values, judgment, professionalism – what have you accomplished by hearing her point of view? What's the baseline for your findings?

A couple of thoughts: Get a grip on who you're talking to, for starters. Identify what the nature of that person's association with the candidate was and is. Are they personal friends? Did they work at the same company 'together,' or did they work *together*-together? Were they peers, or did one manage the other? Was this person a legitimate stakeholder in your candidate's performance? How tightly wrapped is the reference? Is the candidate laid back or perfectionist? Is the reference credible?

Avoid posing questions that can be answered with generalizations. Ask for examples, details and scale. Use a rating system and persist in getting comparisons to others in similar roles. Compare, contrast and compare some more. Numbers are better than letter grades; they're less subjective, somehow. I like the Netflix 1-5 system. Clarify anything less than a '5.' Listen carefully for pauses and awkward silences. Does the candidate have real competencies, or just attributes? Learn what euphemisms are and how to recognize them. Push back. Ask for more examples.

Learn the candidate's job mandates, decisions, consequences, good and bad. Use the word "how" whenever possible. (She split the Red Sea? Really? Please tell me *how* . . . and don't leave anything out!)

Know precisely – not approximately – what type of information you seek. Make sure you have a copy of the job specification in front of you, including desired objectives and outcomes. Are you planning to mold the job around the person or try and squeeze a person into the job? How much creativity and autonomy is built into this position? Always talk in terms of results; then work backwards to understand strategies and tactics used to achieve them. Be certain you know beyond any reasonable doubt whether, when and under what circumstances the reference might want to work with your candidate again. And why.

Now test yourself. Ask the reference if you can call back and review this data once you've organized your notes. If the answer is "No way," you've done a first-rate job. Congratulations.

30

COUNTER-OFFERS RECONSIDERED

So you've accepted a new job and given two weeks' notice to your current employer. Before you have a chance to clean out your desk, here comes the old boss, all warm smiles and reconciliation, proposing that you hang in with a digitally enhanced title, a 20 percent increase in salary and a substantial retention bonus. The comp is now roughly equal between the two gigs, but the satisfaction quotient for staying put is intense. What do you do?

Being on the receiving end of a juicy counter-offer is, for the emotionally needy, the fulfilment of a life's dream. It's like getting an email from that girl you adored in high school – the one who didn't realize you existed – saying she's been haunted by your memory these past 15 years and has remained completely chaste (but still hormonal) in anticipation of your reunion. Or maybe a slightly tipsy call from your ex-wife at 2:00 in the morning where she has to choke back the tears of remorse as she tells you that her new husband is a swine and she just can't erase you from her genetic code. (Stop that some more!) Far be it for me to advise you not to accept a tasty dish of vindication. No excuses or apologies necessary. The occasional gloat can do wonders for your health.

Surely by now you've heard all the standard reasons for being suspicious of an employer who doesn't pay you what you're worth until you give notice. But it might be interesting to freeze-frame the video on that exchange for a second and consider how easily you can be manipulated even though you *think* you're holding all the cards.

Let's examine your state of mind. You logged in, say, five years of hard work and were hoping the payoff would have already appeared. When it didn't, you took a serious overture to its logical conclusion and earned the promotion somewhere else. Although you weren't actively looking, what's a motivated person supposed to do when opportunity knocks? Assume it's a burglar? And it's not just about the money, either. It's about recognition, respect, responsibility . . . the whole enchilada.

What you really want your boss to say is, "Thanks for the great work. I wish we'd shown you more appreciation while we had the chance. You've been terrific and we deserve to lose you. Wherever you go and whatever you do, I'm certain you'll be hugely successful." But instead he merely offers you more dough. And you're tempted to settle for that, minimally, as a substitute for what you really crave: acknowledgement. So in the radiant moment when your boss asks you to stay, as much as you might want to snort derisively and turn your back on him, you can't. It's like that hug your father never gave you. And now you have it. Sort of.

The most dangerous situation is not where you don't know what's going on and are therefore vulnerable. It's where you imagine that you *do* know what's going on but are dead wrong, because you're missing critical information or insight. We now understand this to be the Dunning-Kruger effect.

Well, it's your decision. But please keep in view that you're highly susceptible to being played when you quit, and be aware of the reasons why. Also remember that the place where you pay your dues is often not the same place you'll reap the rewards.

31

WHAT TO DO WHEN YOU COME IN SECOND

Now that corporate hiring is warming again, I've heard from a number of people whose dance cards have become suddenly – and in many cases disappointingly – full. They're being courted, all right, but wind up "always a bridesmaid, never a bride." While serial close calls may validate your credentials and credibility as a candidate in an exceptionally competitive and still nervous job market, it's also frustrating as hell. Is there nothing you can do about it?

Interview skills are not the same as work skills. This cannot be said often enough. Based on my own unscientific observations, the most common error that hiring entities make is to place way too high a premium on a candidate's demonstrated enthusiasm to get the job, and not enough on that person's motivation to actually *do* the job.

Think dating and marriage: two completely different sets of competencies, right? You could launch a convincing argument that the best characteristics of each are incompatible – mutually exclusive, even – with the other. That person who was *sooooo* exciting to be with, who swept you off your feet in a whirlwind of Hollywood-style romance, never once letting you catch your breath . . . can you see him taking out the garbage or helping with the dishes? Probably not. Likewise the stable, loyal, nurturing, and empathic life partner with a sturdy sense of responsibility is very possibly the most boring date in the world. (She'll always be there for you, though. Chicken soup, anyone?)

Preparing, rehearsing and polishing one's interview material – on top of having done the necessary research – generally result in a strong audition. But unless you're interviewing for a position as a full-time interviewee, these talents have little or nothing to do with the role for which you're being hired. Being an extrovert is super-helpful in winning the votes of confidence you need to get the offer. It may not provide any miracles, though, when it comes time for your performance review.

On the rare occurrence when we've talked to a prospective client and the client ultimately decides to hire another search firm (it happens), we like to follow up in a couple of months and see how their search is progressing. What we usually discover is that the other firm was much better than us when it came to marketing themselves, but not so impressive when it came to execution. We pick up a fair amount of business that way, on the rebound from competitors who are all talk and very little walk.

So, if you were runner-up for a position you knew was right in your sweet spot, what do you have to lose by calling the hiring manager 90 days later and asking how that new hotshot is working out? You may be surprised to learn that she wishes she had gone with you, the boring date . . . the one who doesn't mind changing an occasional diaper.

Just a suggestion. Because you never know what might happen.

32

TEN THINGS TO DO WHEN PEOPLE DISAPPOINT YOU

If you've been reading this book diligently, it may have come to your attention that I can be a bit critical. Okay, fair call. It's not that I *dislike* people . . . I'm just not a super-huge fan. Plus, I get paid to figure out where their weaknesses are. Lately, in my spare time, I've been thinking about practical ways to deal with the oh-so-common feeling of crushing disappointment that comes when others inevitably let you down.

As you certainly learned by the age of four or five, people will let you down repeatedly and consistently, through deeds of commission and omission. Am I overstating the case? Don't think so. They will lie, mock, embarrass, mislead, provoke, double-cross, slander and make thoughtless errors in judgment that hurt you terribly. Hey, what do you expect? They're human! The worst part, though, is not the casual matter-of-factness with which they do these things. It's that they do them to *you*. And the challenge then becomes deciding what to do about it.

Here's a multiple-choice menu I developed to help you explore options for reacting to this ongoing dilemma. You may want to select more than one category in any given circumstance, as all items are subject to change based on setting, diet and mood. Enjoy!

Throw a tantrum. Sometimes people don't fathom how serious the situation is, or how badly they've failed you . . . until you scream loudly. Forget abstractions. Show them in real time by acting out your rage and sense of betrayal. They'll thank you for the clarity! Don't forget to hurl a few extra-spicy epithets while you're at it. Preparation and rehearsal are key to successful execution. Practice in front of a mirror or a friend, if you have one.

Pout. Perhaps you were told otherwise as a child, but most folks really love this. It's adorable . . . and effective! Just pretend that you're Mommy's little prince or Daddy's little princess and see what happens. You can be angry without having to justify yourself or even admit to any feelings at all. No one gets his wishes met more quickly than the pouter. Stay the course and they'll eventually come around.

Condescend. Another time-honored strategy that will have your intended recipient dizzy with contrition. Superior is good; haughty is even better. Speak to the person as if he or she were mentally impaired. Ask for explanations and then respond by saying, "I don't understand. Can you explain it again?" Interrupt whenever possible. Make 'em squirm, back 'em up against the wall and squish 'em like helpless bugs. Then see how hard they try to win back your respect.

Get even. Warm or cold, revenge is a delicious treat. Cook up a batch and watch the remorse eat away at your tormentor. There are so many different ways to inflict pain and humiliation . . . tantalizing choices all. You can punish your victim in secret or out in the open for everyone to see. Experiment and have fun with it!

Criticize. Whether it's directly to people's faces or behind their back, this classic response will never go out of style. The more ridiculous they look, the more vindication you'll feel. Brush up on the insults and let them fly.

Get stoned. Have a drink, smoke, snort or capsule. Numb those frazzled nerve endings and simply dull the pain. No one appreciates you anyway, right?

Pontificate and intellectualize. It doesn't matter what you say. What matters is that you can define everything on your own terms. Keep talking until their ears bleed.

Ignore them. A personal favorite of mine, nothing sends a clear message like putting on the big chill. If you don't acknowledge people, they cease to exist. Problem solved!

Keep your head down and do your job. No commentary required. That's life.

Get over it.

33

NO ONE IS BETTER THAN ANYONE

Many years ago, my wife hired a housekeeper who had emigrated some time earlier from Russia. She was in her late fifties and highly educated, having been a language and music teacher in the former Soviet Union. I had fun teaching her American idioms and watching her break stuff.

Ella was sweet and eager to please, but she came with a serious set of cultural limitations. As a random example, she once left the baby unattended – conspicuously in a carriage out on the front lawn – while busy with a project inside the house. It was a warm day, after all. The only thing she forgot to do was put out a 'Free Baby' sign next to him.

Then there was her total lack of familiarity with basic cleaning and household products, the kind we have in this country. So I might find her using Comet on the kitchen floor, or Windex on the mahogany bookcase, or Murphy Oil Soap on . . . well, you get the idea. I tried in vain to convince my wife to find a better solution, but she kept insisting that Ella wasn't so bad. At least we had *someone*. (And who else, she was quick to point out, would want to work for me?)

Finally, after months of procrastination, we did let Ella go to another family in the neighborhood – they spoke fluent Russian, bless their hearts – and we hired a seasoned pro who grew up in Wisconsin. (It's not about the country of origin, by the way; it's about the skill set.) Cathy's been with us 15 years now and most mornings I can't find the Alka-Seltzer without her help.

With Ella we had, like, *half* a housekeeper. When the inconvenience of hiring a new person was looming – or we simply lacked the urgency to pursue other options – it was easy to fall back on the idea that a living, breathing human showed up for work each day. Once she was gone, however, the path to action was clear and unambiguous. In other words, *having no housekeeper was actually better than having half a housekeeper* . . . because with no housekeeper, we realized that we needed to hire one.

Corporations drag their feet exactly like this more often than anyone cares to admit. The resulting irony is that while millions of good people are unemployed or under-employed right now, lots of marginal and mediocre performers stay in place at every level of an organization because it's just too much hassle to replace them. Hmmmm . . . kinda makes you wonder about the half-glass thingy, doesn't it?

Moral of the story: Don't let the half obscure the void.

34

HOW DO YOU DEFINE SUCCESS REALLY?

Independent of what motivates you, how you think about money, whether you tend to capitalize on your strengths or protect your weak spots . . . how will you ultimately grade yourself on overall career success? Will it be based on how long you stayed in the game? The level of influence or recognition you achieved? What about the quality and durability of your relationships? Personally meaningful and satisfying accomplishments? Financial security? Respect?

While enjoying my morning coffee, I generally read the obituaries. These concise little profiles of the recently deceased interest me for a number of reasons (truly, what better way to begin the day than by not seeing your own name?) and I'm hardly the first to appreciate them as a bona fide literary form.

It seems as if there's a bit of competition going on from beyond the grave, too. Numbers of children, grandchildren and surviving spouses offer a snapshot of how the subjects surrounded themselves with others, assuring the reader that they were seldom, if ever, lonely. Details of education, military or community service, career achievements and leisure pursuits help us recognize a life lived to its fullest – or one cut tragically short. And unless it's just me, I think there's also a reflection, a natural process of self-comparison that goes on when we read them. We wonder or speculate what our own obituaries might look like and how our own descriptions will measure up . . . or not.

Let me go out on a limb for a second and say that comparison is a terrible thing. Rather than inspiring us to greatness, it cripples our ability to learn and grow by warping our perspective. Of course it's also fundamental to our culture, upbringing and education – woven into the fabric of one's early identity. There's nothing better than competition for driving a free-market economy, but for the individual, it's psychological poison.

Observe for an hour a day, if you can, how much of your total thought process is the by-product of constant comparison and judgment. You may even discover that many of your opinions are merely defenses, insurance policies against feeling inferior or inadequate in someone else's eyes. Such a huge piece of what we think, say, and do is based on comparing ourselves with others and competing for the Big Prize . . . which is often hidden behind the curtain marked 'Fame.' Or so we're inclined to believe.

Now imagine that you're 80 and looking back on a lifetime of activity. Examine your professional life for a moment and be completely honest about what matters to you . . . not what you think you *should* want, but what you really care about deeply. However much money you earned in your career, lots of folks made more. Yup, it's true. Even though you probably put an ocean of time and effort and discipline into earning a livelihood, thousands (perhaps millions) who were less motivated, less energetic, less intelligent, less savvy – who worked less and planned less and sacrificed less – made much, much more. Some people starved, too, but you're not so worried about them. You're concerned about the ones who did 'better' than you, the regrets and lost opportunities. Why?

Whether your job is running a $20 billion corporation, clearing the debris from logging trails in Oregon or providing collagen injections for needy, thin-lipped patients in Beverly Hills, there will always be somebody who does it better, faster, more artfully or for bigger profits. Does that mean you're a loser? Does even the word 'loser' make you wince?

Are you good at making money, or simply good at what you do? How do you fulfill yourself? Is it all relative? (Speaking of relatives . . . do you still need your parents' approval, or have you moved on?)

Seriously . . . will you even know if you win your own contest?

35

WHAT KEEPS YOU GOING BESIDES COFFEE?

If your portfolio is flat and your career prospects have darkened, it's possible that being thrown headfirst into the jungle has magically transformed you into a tiger. As Lance Armstrong once said, "Through my illness I learned rejection. I was written off. That was the moment I thought, 'Game on. No prisoners. Everybody is going down.'"

Or possibly not. Lance doesn't sound quite human, did you say? All that chest-thumping makes you want to curl up on the sofa and take a nap? Maybe, like zillions of others, you've just misplaced your mojo in the fray. Don't be embarrassed. Motivation is a big issue – always has been – particularly for those of us who grew up without having to worry if there's going to be any food on the table.

How do you work up the conviction and discipline you need to do tiresome, unglamorous tasks? How do you get yourself through high school, college, a boring job? And what about those years after you figure out that you're probably not going to conquer the world?

Most of us reject the idea of leading lives of quiet desperation. But it could be time to re-examine what's important to you professionally, aside from the obvious need to earn a living, and to quit trying to live up to someone else's standards for achievement. Whether you're out interviewing and are asked to articulate your ideals, or getting close to a decision about an opportunity that's currently on the table, identifying core motivators in basic, simplistic terms might prove useful. The same set of criteria can also help you better understand co-workers and job candidates.

In no particular order, here are the primary elements I've observed over years of interviewing.

Money. Total compensation, including cash and non-cash items. It's not so much what the money buys, usually, as what the money *means* – psychologically and socially. Beware the individual who puts this at the top of his or her list. Will that person bolt for an extra few dollars?

Status. In short, this where you stand on the org chart or totem pole. How many people do you have to bow down to versus how many kneel at your feet? Executives often have great difficulty admitting, even to themselves, just how important this is to them.

Prestige. What level of eminence, reputation and public esteem does your company enjoy? For example, would you rather be a senior vice president at Wal-Mart . . . or a vice president at Nordstrom's? Everything else being equal, that is.

Culture. This is about people, camaraderie, shared values and belonging. Are you proud and happy to be a member of this group? Would you want to spend, say, Thanksgiving with them?

Autonomy. To what extent do you define the goals and objectives for your function? Is Big

Brother watching . . . or have you been given the self-determination to succeed on your own lights?

Wow Factor. This could be anything from the coolest technology in the world to being located in the same town as your new romantic interest. In other words, any consideration that overrides the factors mentioned above. Do you want to bring your boss coffee and doughnuts? No? What if your boss is Steven Spielberg? You get it now.

Rank the categories in order of personal priority and try to guess what the sequence might be for those who irritate or confound you. Seeing yourself and others through these lenses could bring a new degree of clarity to the mystery of why people behave as they do at the office – including that rascal in the mirror. Try to observe without judging and see how many of these levers you can recognize in action.

One more word on the subject of motivation. Being a professional doesn't mean you have to be inspired in everything you do. It means playing at the top of your game and performing *as if* you were inspired. That's not about trying to conceal the fact that your heart maybe isn't completely in it at all times, but doing great work *despite* it. So even if you are just going through the motions, don't forget the motions.

36

THE SECRET MEANING
OF MONEY

Super-affluent people aren't like us. Oh, sure, they eat and sleep and reproduce and die like everyone else. Yet somewhere along the way – regardless of how they were raised, it seems – the ultra-rich acquired the elusive Wealthy gene. You and I *could* have it, but basically we just don't.

Countless books have been written on the subject of how to develop and nurture the gene. It's tricky, though. One major problem is that you have to read at least three or four chapters of pretty dull material before getting to the main points. And even then, it's often buried in a lot of boring other stuff. So here's the bottom line up top (and please remember me as the guy who didn't waste your time): For obscenely loaded individuals, money is just money. And making it is a game.

Obviously, you and I have a whole different set of conditioning from childhood. Money, the way it usually is for us middle class-types (unless, like the precious few, we become liberated and enlightened), always *means* something. How we earn it, who we have to serve to get it, the degree of basic dignity our role permits, the voice in which we get to speak, the mask or costume we have to wear. Those are only a few of the metrics around money for us. They also include being needed and valued and appreciated and respected and all that emotional crap. I *know* . . . right?

Here's a prime example. Why does a job candidate turn down a job offer at $195,000 but accept one at $200,000? After taxes, the difference is negligible. What can someone at that level of income possibly buy with $5,000 that he or she couldn't afford without it? You know the answer: It's not what the money buys. It's what the money means. The round number has a special meaning that the other one doesn't convey. Because the candidate – like most of us – lacks an essential gene, which, if we had it, would gently remind us that money is just money.

Clearly one of the most devastating effects of the economic downturn has come in the form of ego deflation; namely, the crushing realization that 'career yardage gained" can be reversed in the blink of eye. While people believed they had turned an important corner or pulled themselves over a hump or matriculated to the next level in their professional trajectories, there was, in fact, no corner, no hump or level. Such images exist only in Dungeons and Dragons. Practically speaking, these are nothing more than self-sustaining stories we tell ourselves as we lumber toward the ultimate finish line: retirement. So the myth of building on past income and accomplishments is a limitation to be overcome. And the very rich get this.

That's why we can get close to 'comfortable, thanks" but still not become Wealthy. People who have the Wealthy gene aren't necessarily addicted to luxury or think they're above the rest of the world. They're not hungrier and I don't believe they work any harder. Financial independence materializes for them precisely because it is all a big game, because money is just money (you have to keep repeating that in order to get your head around it) and because it doesn't matter how or where they earn it (Wall Street or Walmart, no difference) or what denomination it comes in, as long as it's more or less honorable and they don't leave anything on the table when they go home for dinner.

So we're kinda messed up in that way. Psychologically, I mean. No, seriously. The very rich are totally healthy and we are messed up. Money is just money in the Major Leagues, and possibly everyone who ever earned a giant boatload of it had to learn that lesson first.

Whatever. At least we'll always have our youthful figures.

37

WHY DID THE CONSULTANT CROSS THE ROAD?

Does anyone work at companies anymore? It's not clear. Going strictly by anecdotal data and an endless stream of recent emails, it appears that every third or fourth person over the age of 19 is some type of consultant. Not that there's anything wrong with that. *I'm* a consultant (although whether I'd want my son or daughter to marry one is another subject). But it feels a bit crowded suddenly, with uncertain boundaries, kind of like a hot tub after the neighbors drop by and the water becomes tepid and brackish.

If there was a bona fide workforce trend sweeping the country – one similar to the great migration from rural to industrial enterprise that took place a century ago – a trend whereby we'd abandon legacy organizational design methods and move towards a more cost-effective pay-per-play model, let's say, I'd totally get that. (We do see it happening here and there on wobbly baby steps with mixed results.)

What I'm referring to, though, is not lean or virtual teams aggregated under a single banner and dedicated to common goals, where you outsource IT, maybe, or HR. I'm talking about the tens of thousands (possibly millions) of people who are now available to advise you on anything from creating and marketing your 'personal brand' to navigating social media to learning how not to roll your eyes when employees ask for a raise. My favorite, of course, is the high-profile intuitive who for a mere ten grand per month will tell you whether your strategies *feel* right.

At the bottom of a desk drawer in my office is a business card that reads, 'Waiter/Consultant'. And why not? What have those big corporations done for us lately? Perhaps very soon in this economically ravaged, post-apocalyptic era we'll all wind up joining little bands of nomadic consultants, bartering with other tribes for the necessities of life as we drift without compass in search of physical and spiritual sustenance.

The sub-specialty that truly amazes me is executive coaches. Would someone please do a quick DNA check on these individuals? Are they highly experienced, savvy former captains of industry who decided to share their career insights with the rest of humanity out of sheer love for the capitalist system? Have they indeed spent the better part of their professional lives observing, parsing and categorizing executive behaviors, documenting with painful precision what works and what doesn't, presumably as part of a well-known group like McKinsey? Are they former instructors at the Harvard or the Wharton school of business? Are they available for the occasional landscaping project?

Even more perplexing is this: When did every living executive get diagnosed as being in critical need of coaching? I missed that memo. And how did all these dysfunctional leaders manage to fool so many people for so long? How were they able to last as much as fifteen minutes given the extreme darkness that surrounds them as they stumble cluelessly through their surrealistic dream worlds?

There are coaches to help you, as a manager, communicate more effectively. Coaches can unlock and develop your Emotional Intelligence, which apparently is now a must, gracious living-wise. There are coaches who will teach you how to increase the productivity of your employees, how to figure out what role suits you best, how to identify interpersonal issues from your past that might be interfering with your management style, how to get along with an irrational boss (he needs some serious coaching, too) and how to build more loyal and effective teams. Say . . . how did you ever get hired in the first place, I wonder? We'll have to assume your cousin owns the company. Or that you slept your way to the top. Probably both.

When your coaching regimen is complete, you may realize that management is not really your thing. Possibly you'll be honest enough to admit to yourself and others that you're not cut out for corporate life after all. Chances are then you'll discover a whole new career path, one that allows you the freedom and autonomy you never had by not tying you down to arbitrary goals and rigid objectives. I know! You can become a consultant.

38

THE FINE ART OF DELIVERING BAD NEWS

It's no longer considered best practice in corporations to sneak up behind employees and tell them they're fired. Delivering what are now called 'difficult messages' has become something of an art form, and understanding how to shoot a person with conspicuous empathy is known as Emotional Intelligence.

Clearly what matters is *how* you deliver the message. A recent survey reveals that employees prefer form over substance pretty much every time. Do it right and expect to see high-fives all around when you announce that the company was just bought by a German consortium. The whole 'I have good news and bad news' thing is over, too, by the way. And don't sweat that small stuff because it's *all* good news. Division moving to the Ukraine? Use the right facial expression, body language and cologne and you can send them packing with glee.

The true test of whether a supervisor has mastered the Tao of delivering difficult messages comes when a staff member must be let go, regardless of the reason. Those who conduct the process are asked to be aware of their own personal feelings about the recipient and may, on occasion, need to suppress the urge to break into song. The ability to read subtle non-verbal cues and diffuse various neural alarms in others is equally vital. The practical application of these techniques might include offering a tissue at the appropriate moment, responding with a sorrowful glance or empathic sigh or simply learning to cope with the appearance of automatic weapons.

A fascinating study conducted by a leading human resource consulting group indicates that certain follow-up questions may be useful in helping the discharged individual achieve closure. The benevolent terminator should ask: How well did I listen? How would you rate my resonance with your pain? Did I speak your name often enough, pronounce it correctly and say it in a caring tone? Would you want to use me if you were being fired again? Would you recommend that I fire one of your colleagues or friends?

Skilled managers will not only have the soon-to-be-jobless in their emotional court, as it were, but actually cheering their performances. Above all, the downsized person should be chipper enough to sit up and answer the exit interviewer's most important question: 'Was it good for *you*?"

I've always said that it's best to achieve total enlightenment by 30 so you can get on with other projects. Sadly, not everyone listens to my advice. And that's where people run into big problems.

The philosophy that has eased me through the awkward moments of interpersonal transactions is this: Shoot them in the head, not the body. I'm convinced that genuine compassion – the milk of human kindness – requires putting grownups out of their misery as early in the game as possible by giving them the straight scoop. This doesn't mean it has to be brutal. Just the opposite. It should be clean, dignified and . . . well, the word that comes to mind is 'elegant.'

Imagine Spencer Tracy in the role of, say, a hard-driving, hard-drinking newspaper editor who has to tell a newsboy that his dog has been run over by one of the company's delivery trucks. How would Tracy do it? Why, he'd rub that lovable, craggy old face with his meaty paw, pull his lower lip for poise and say, "Kid, there's no easy way to put this. Your pooch is flatter than Monday's late edition."

Tracy and I are similar in many ways, all of them flattering. In my role as an executive recruiter, I have honed the communication of difficult messages to a level of proficiency that has made me the envy of radiologists and college admission officers alike. Candidates are sensitive, and it should come as no surprise that the more senior the executive, the more diplomacy is indicated. Just tell a person who earns $1.2 million that he blew an interview and watch his eyes cloud with tears. It's almost enough to break your heart.

That's precisely why the blow must be swift and merciful. No second-guessing when I say, "My client hated your attitude" or "Someone else is getting the offer." And no confusion when I administer the kindest cut of all: "We'll call you if something else comes up."

39

THE MYTH OF CORPORATE CULTURE

You may have surmised by now that I am firmly opposed to public disembowelment. In most cases. An exception can be made for the snake-oil salesman who first peddled the notion that corporations should have adorable personalities.

Saying that companies have a 'corporate culture' is like saying that Ivan the Terrible had a 'management style.' How can a multinational conglomerate with 47,000 employees in a dozen countries claim a common culture? How about an enterprise where nine different languages are spoken on the production floor and senior management can barely speak any?

What we mostly experience in business is a systemic pathology, often nothing more than a constantly shifting aggregation of *disparate behaviors*. Corporate culture began as a fairy tale back in the quaint, bygone eras when middle-aged White Guys ruled the planet (trust me, I've seen the fossils) . . . and it remains so today.

The idea that a work environment has been purposefully constructed to guarantee specific outcomes is perfectly reasonable. Instill competencies? You betcha. Deliver efficiencies, even. But can it produce unifying mythologies and customs? Don't think so. Certainly no art, music or literature.

I understand how people might confuse culture with *brand*, particularly if they still get goose bumps listening to "I'd Like to Teach the World to Sing." My neighbor Patrick Hanlon wrote an

interesting book, *Primal Branding*, explaining the
seven key components upon which larger-than-life
corporate brands are built:

1. Creation story (like in the Bible)

2. Creed (as in "this is the Cubs' year")

3. Rituals (banging drums in the sweat lodge)

4. Icons (dazzling the senses, from coffee to
   doughnuts)

5. Sacred words ("grande decaf latte, please")

6. Pagans (who refuse to drink the Kool-Aid)

7. Fearless Leader (from Buddha to Welch)

That's how you create a juggernaut consumer
brand. Entirely different thing, culture.

Since the label 'culture' is so nebulous, it can
conveniently mask or whitewash the true
underlying beliefs and behaviors of any group,
ranging from hospitality to bestiality. I prefer the
more pedestrian term 'values'. Beliefs combined
with behaviors equal values.

The values of a group might be honorable – or
not. Unlike the mushier name culture, with its
connotation of a cozy melting pot or a delightfully
harmonious salad bowl, *values* includes more than
what is outwardly professed, endlessly parroted
and tritely canonized on T-shirts and coffee mugs.
It also encompasses what is implicit, often
deliberately buried and denied. People may talk
your ear off about their culture, but values can be
seen in real-time . . . as evidenced by real actions.

In my work as a recruiter, it helps me to think of companies as big, messy families with varying degrees of dysfunction – despite the many talents and productive output of its members. In this context, the challenge becomes less of matching cultures than of elevating values; bearing in mind, of course, how resistant systems are to anything other than mild, incremental change. But that's another set of encyclopedias I'll come back later to show you.

Meanwhile, the question CEOs may want to ask their executive teams is this: "How should we behave among ourselves and with customers to give us the best chance of achieving our business objectives?"

Who knows? The right responses might even breed some culture.

40

CHOOSE BETTER HABITS AND ENJOY THEM LESS

Having misspent most of my youth in questionable pursuits, it feels weird to suggest a few items that might appear . . . well, *wholesome*. Possibly Spartan. Dweebish, even. Believe me, it's not my intention to moralize. But if the sprint has turned into a marathon and you're an old dog looking to keep up with a bunch of young pups, perhaps one of these ideas might help. Or not. Totally your call.

Get up before the sun. No practice could ever feel more bizarre and unnatural, particularly to yours truly. But it's the right thing to do and you know it. Every successful person since the advent of opposable thumbs has risen at the crack of butt. Set your alarm for the same ridiculous time each day and get moving.

Guard your tongue. What are your motives when you speak? To control? To impress? Are you always truthful? Sincere? How much of what you say is gossip and rumor? I realize it sounds harsh, but verbal mischief is our reality, isn't it? Imagine that all your remarks are being permanently recorded in an email and sent around to every person you know, that people *never* keep anything you tell them in confidence (they don't, by the way) and that privacy only exists inside your head. It usually costs nothing to say nothing. Gain mastery over this secret weapon and you will become powerful beyond your wildest dreams. Don't take my word for it – test it yourself.

Eat less. Get a divorce from those evil twins, sugar and carbs. Skip the breakup sex and go directly for the restraining order. Seriously, it's not that difficult. Stick with protein and use smaller amounts of everything. (It's your emotions that want feeding, not your body.) Also, see if you can survive without eating for two or three hours before going to sleep. That's the hardest part by far, but it pays off with handsome dividends. In a few short months you'll actually be the correct size and shape. Then go buy some clothes that fit.

What, me worry? Have you not figured this out yet? Whatever the concerns – money, health, children, the future – and no matter how legitimate your need to panic, stressing and obsessing will only paralyze you. Yes, life can and often does blow giant chunks. But has gunning the fear engine ever done anything to relieve the pain? When you worry, you're just recycling the past. This is now. Extricate yourself and do something useful.

Quit sucking up. Totally not kidding here. In fact, you should consider giving up manipulation entirely. Flattery, appeasement and old-fashioned bootlicking are especially poisonous to a relationship . . . even if your manager is a modern-day Caligula. Oh, I know you think it'll hurt your career. That's only because you haven't mastered the alternatives. But combine it with the verbal continence mentioned above and you may find yourself being given more responsibility and rewards than ever before. The trick to dealing with larger-than-life people who rule your destiny is this: Never suck up, but remember that the conversation is always about *their* issues, not yours.

Don't be sanctimonious. Hey, what's the weather like up there on Mount Olympus? Nobody can stand that crap, so just don't start. If you believe in tolerance, kindly extend your tolerance to include those who are intolerant. Right? And while we're on the subject, can the phony humility. When you become great, then you can act humble.

Do like a Boy Scout. A scout is trustworthy, loyal, helpful, friendly, courteous, kind, obedient, cheerful, thrifty, brave, clean and reverent. Need I say more?

There's no guarantee that you'll derive any pleasure from these new habits, as I'm sure you are aware. But they could keep you in the game and competitive. My father used to tell the story about a man who sought the advice of a Himalayan guru in his quest to live forever.

"Stay away from tobacco, alcohol and women," the guru told him.

"Really?" the man asked. "And then I'll live forever?"

"Well, no," said the guru. "But it'll seem like it."

CPSIA information can be obtained at www.ICGtesting.com
Printed in the USA
BVOW05*1530281214

379999BV00002B/4/P